D1765767

Power Training for Combat, MMA, Boxing, Wrestling, Martial Arts, and Self-Defense

How to Develop Knockout Punching Power, Kicking Power, Grappling Power, and Ground Fighting Power

Version 1.0

By J. Barnes

Legal Notice

Disclaimer

Table of Contents

Introduction

Getting Started
With Power Training

Thank you for purchasing this book. I have written this guide with a single objective in mind--to help you become a superior fighter by increasing your combat power to the highest level of your innate potential.

Power is a key attribute for success in self-defense and competitive fighting. Knockout power is often the great equalizer in a fight as it can quickly turn the tables and deliver a definitive victory for the well-trained knockout specialist.

The fighter who is known to possess knockout power gains immediate confidence and instills instant respect in his opponent.

Do you wish to have the power of great knockout fighters and combat champions? Are you in need of the latest training science and tools to help you develop more explosive strikes, takedowns, and submissions? If so, this guide is for you.

Power is often an elusive, mysterious, and revered attribute for the beginning combat student. But, this guide will break it down for you so that you can fully grasp the fundamentals and critical insights that will help you develop and maximize your knockout and submission power.

I have seen and fought many technically capable fighters. Some were very elaborate in their techniques, but if they lacked power--I would simply blow right through their impressive array of movements with a succession of power shots, knowing that it would only take one connection to abruptly end the fight.

Having crippling power at your disposal provides you with increased confidence when going into any physical confrontation. Your opponent becomes cautious, if not downright afraid, when he senses or feels a small bit of real knockout power.

After reading this guide, you will know how to train for combat power, regardless of your size or current strength levels. All you need to do is commit to the training methods in this book. When you put the information in this book into action, you will double your striking and submission power, and increase your ability to win fights by knockout or tap out.

What You Will Find in This Guide

It is my belief—based on studying the most effective and successful fighters—that maximizing power (and fighting skill) is the direct result of the following five essentials.

1. Knowledge
2. Guidance
3. Tools
4. Motivation
5. Action

In this guide--I will provide information, insights, innovations, and inspiration on all five essentials—for the purpose of helping you *maximize your combat power proficiency*.

This book is divided into ten chapters. The following is a brief description of the contents for each chapter.

Chapter 1: The Knockout and Submission. You will learn more about the highly touted (and often elusive) knockout. Learn the science behind knockout and submission power and gain more knowledge about the process and physiological causes.

Chapter 2: Combat PowerSync™. You will learn about an innovative and little-known concept that is employed by all great knockout fighters. Combat PowerSync is the key to unlocking your innate power potential. You can develop the ability to relay destructive power quickly and consistently in a variety of ways to help control and finish fights.

Chapter 3: Power Principles. Learn the seven fundamental principles of combat power. No dominant fighter ignores these immutable principles of power fighting. With this knowledge, you will have a good starting point for building the foundation of your power training program.

Chapter 4: Power Attributes. Discover the most important attributes for developing knockout power and increasing your wins. While power principles are the foundation of your knowledge base, the attributes covered in this chapter are the building blocks of your combat power development.

Chapter 5: Strikes, Takedowns, Chokes, and Locks. In order to attack or counter your opponent with maximum power, you will need to use proven techniques or power weapons. Based on statistics and experience, these are the "go-to" weapons" for power fighters—because they deliver consistent knockouts and submissions.

Chapter 6: Power Training Tools. Every great fighter or champion athlete understands the importance of training tools for maximizing skills and performance. Due in large part to continuous improvements in training tools and science, athletes in general (and fighters specifically) continue to get better with each successive generation. This critical chapter covers the specific training equipment that you will use to develop superior power attributes and skills in the shortest possible time.

Chapter 7: Supplemental Power Training. Learn how to leverage the latest supplemental training methods to keep your body and mind in tiptop condition. Scientific studies have proven that these supplemental tools will improve your combat power capacity and total fighting effectiveness.

Chapter 8: Avoiding The Knockout and Submission. Developing the ability to win fights by knockout will teach you a lot about how to manage (and respect) combat power. This chapter continues your combat power education by teaching you how to avoid being knocked out by power shots or taken down and defeated by powerful submissions.

Chapter 9: Power Training Program. This pivotal section pulls everything together to give you a successful jumpstart in your combat power training.

Using simple and convenient tools--you will learn how to plan, execute, and adapt your training sessions for continuous improvements.

Chapter 10: Combat Power Inspiration. Developing knockout power requires commitment, education, and training. In this chapter, I break down the power styles of the greatest knockout fighters. Plus, you will learn how to assemble a *combat power team*, increase your power IQ, and maintain your training motivation.

How to Get Your Money's Worth From This Book

You should not just read this guide and put it aside once you are done. I am your consultant, and this guide is the beginning of a two-way conversation between you, who wants to become a superior fighter by maximizing your total power, and me, who is providing the essential information that will help you achieve your goal.

I believe that this guide is unlike any other ever published on the subject of power training for combat. By breaking down all of the key components of power and relying on science and the experience of current and past knockout artists, this guide can help you double or triple your power in punching, kicking, throwing, and grappling.

This guide is designed to help fighters from all combat backgrounds, including boxing, MMA, martial arts, self-defense, and wrestling. You should adapt the information as you see fit to get the most out of this guide based on your combat goals.

As a combat student, you must take action (commit, learn, train) before you can get results. If you follow this guide and train consistently, I guarantee you will see significant improvement in your power and fighting skills.

For starters, I suggest you browse through the book to get a sense of its contents. From there, you should study one chapter at a time. The chapters are in a specific order to progressively build your Combat PowerSync.

After reading each chapter, you should reflect, make highlights, and take notes. Once you are finished reading the book, you will be ready to start training. However, do not jump right into the drills. Superior combat students do not waste training time! So, make sure you have a solid plan before you start (don't worry, I'll show you how to develop the ideal power training program).

You will get the most from this guide, or any other, by continuously following these five steps:

1. Know your definite purpose or goal.

2. With an open mind, study the material thoroughly.

3. Use everything that is beneficial to your purpose or goal.

4. Ignore everything that is useless to your purpose or goal.

5. Apply the modified insights on a focused and consistent basis to realize your purpose or goal in the shortest possible time.

A Few Words About Me and My Role in Your Life

I have studied and participated in various combat systems and sports for more than 20 years. During those years, I have gone through many physical and mental transformations. Every one of those transformations has been for the better, because I am constantly striving to improve my knowledge, capabilities, and effectiveness.

Sometimes I take two steps forward and one step back, but over time, I am moving forward and progressing. I encourage you to focus on consistent progress in order to reach your full potential as a fighter and combat student.

I grew up spending a lot of time on rough city streets, which lead me to being in many real street fights. I have studied many forms of combat, including reality-based martial arts, traditional martial arts, boxing, wrestling, and MMA. I have never initiated a street fight, but I was able to win all but one of the fights by knockout. Luckily, I am still here to tell the story (and I encourage you to avoid street fights, unless you are defending yourself).

My oldest brother introduced me to the martial arts. Once I started training, I became hooked on developing my fighting abilities. I was particularly interested in developing speed and power, as I saw them as critical attributes for surviving a street fight (hit the attacker first--and hit the attacker with enough force to stop him).

As my knockout skills improved, I continued to devour all the information I could find on power training. I trained with fighters from various styles (and of different skills levels) in order to test and develop my theories and methods for maximizing power.

To this day, I continue to train with a wide variety of partners (from beginner to elite champions) in order to stay up-to-date on the latest advancements in combat training.

Don't fall victim to demonstrations of speed or power (I did in the beginning). If the power or speed can't be applied, it is utterly useless in real combat. You want the truth--and I promise you that I will be as brutally honest as I can be about the realities (and myths) of developing knockout power for combat competition and self-defense.

If you ever have any questions about improving your power training, feel free to contact me. I will do my best to provide you with helpful information, in the form of immediate answers, or possibly an entirely new guide. Fair enough?

Okay, enough about that--now let's get started on your combat power training.

Power Training Tip

To develop awe-inspiring power, you must *learn to enjoy contact training!* You simply cannot develop knockout power by punching, kicking, throwing, and grappling with air. One of the most valuable things you will learn from contact training (with a tool or partner) is that you have to penetrate the target in order to cause disruption and damage. When training for power, concentrate on forcefully going *through* the target—and not just making contact with the target.

Chapter 1

The Knockout
and Submission

The Home Run of Fighting

The one-punch knockout or K.O. has been heralded since the beginning of man. It represents the ultimate display of brute force and power in combat. To be able to use your bodily weapons to incapacitate an opponent with one technique is the ultimate in empty hand fighting.

In sports like boxing and MMA--fans clamor for the knockout victory. Who wants to see a long, drawn out decision fight when you can witness the excitement of a T.K.O. win replete with power striking and wrenching submissions from two champions at the peak of their skills? These intense "power battle" fights are usually the profile for "fight of the year" candidates and honors.

The knockout is the home run of fighting. A boxing jab is efficient and beautiful to watch when executed with speed and precision (check out Muhammad Ali in his prime). But, the jab is like a single hit in baseball when compared to a home run.

A vicious left hook, crushing right cross, suffocating rear naked choke, or bone jarring body slam—these weapons are combat home runs because of their force and potential to incapacitate an opponent. Knockouts (like home runs) don't come easy or often for most fighters. However, your goal (and the purpose of this guide) is to develop your ability to win by knockout.

Through commitment and focus on becoming a knockout power fighter--you are more likely to acquire the knowledge, attributes, skills, and instincts to execute a knockout when the opportunity arises during a fight. A word of caution: I hope that you will act responsibly and only use your knockout skills in a legal and appropriate manner, such as for combat sports or self-defense.

Power Defined

According to physics, power equals weight (mass) multiplied by speed (velocity). The corresponding equation is P=WxS (power equals weight x speed).

Another way to define this is power equals work (displacement force) divided by time (speed or velocity). The quantity of work (amount of power) is determined by how much displacement (damage) is caused by the force (weight x speed).

A more powerful punch or kick is one that has more force to create greater displacement (think of the opponent's head snapping back, or the heavy bag swinging backward after being struck with a powerful blow).

Some fighters are more powerful because they are capable of doing *the same amount of work in less time*. All other factors being equal—a faster punch is a more powerful punch because it generates more total force.

Some fighters are more powerful because they are capable of doing *more work in the same amount of time*. All other factors being equal—a heavier punch is a more powerful punch because it generates more total force.

Advanced combat power students understand that increasing the total weight behind a strike is critical to improving knockout capabilities. The more you weigh (assuming no reduction in your movement speed), the harder you are *capable* of striking.

However, this doesn't mean that if you are smaller or in a lighter weight class--that you can't deliver enough power to knock out a larger opponent. By fully developing your innate ability to generate and connect with maximum force--you will be able to knock out or incapacitate most opponents, regardless of their size.

If a heavyweight boxer and a lightweight boxer throw a right cross—how do you determine which punch is more powerful? It depends really. We already know that the heavyweight fighter has *potentially* more weight behind his punch. However, we don't know the total *leveraged* weight behind the right cross for each fighter.

Also, we don't know the relative speed of each fighter's punch. If the lightweight is capable of leveraging all of his bodyweight and has greater speed on impact--he may possibly deliver a more powerful punch. This presumes that the heavyweight fighter's punch is slower and/or carries less weight because of poor punching mechanics.

If, on the other hand, the heavyweight fighter leverages all of his bodyweight and punches with equal speed—he will generate more force (power) than the lightweight fighter. Weight classifications in combat sports are necessary because size does matter when it comes to generating power—assuming all other attributes are equal.

The key takeaway is that you will have to improve the speed, weight, or speed *and* weight of your attacks if you want to improve your power (because power = weight x speed). It's true that your size puts some limitations on your total power. However, with proper training, any healthy fighter is capable of developing knockout power.

Knockout and Submission Science

Strikes

The knockout in simple terms is a sudden shock to the brain that renders a temporary state of unconsciousness or incapacitation. Strikes to the face area or torso are capable of causing a knockout.

Knockouts by striking are caused when the force of impact causes the brain to hit the skull and become bruised. This is typically referred to as a concussion. When faced with this traumatic event, the brain may begin to shut down portions of the nervous system as a defensive mechanism to prevent further damage. This process leads to the temporary paralysis and subsequent collapse often seen in knockouts.

The person who is knocked out will often comment that he was not aware of the knockout. In fact, it is common for the knockout victim to experience a "blackout" and not realize he was struck until he regains consciousness after a few seconds.

Given the right circumstances and opponent, everyone is vulnerable to a knockout. Just because one fighter can deliver a knockout strike doesn't make him immune to getting knocked out if the opponent can hit with the same force and precision.

Throws

When throwing an opponent--it is the floor, wall, or other solid object that will cause the damage and potential knockout. Knockout throws are not as common as knockout strikes in combat competition (due to floor and ring padding). However, power throws are *very* effective in self-defense for thwarting a surprise attacker and introducing him to the concrete with extreme force and damaging consequences.

A skilled grappler can execute a knockout power throw or body slam by grabbing and controlling various parts of the opponent's body, including--the head, face, neck, torso, arms, legs, shoulder and hip.

Keep in mind that you will need the same core power qualities of *speed and weight leveraging* in order to knock out an opponent with a power throw or body slam.

Submissions

All wrestling and grappling specialists understand that submissions are just as effective as strikes and throws for rendering an opponent unconscious or incapacitated. A well-executed power choke, or joint wrenching can cause unbearable pain and deliver a win very quickly for the skilled submission fighter.

Submission vital targets--sought out by all power grapplers--include the neck, elbow, and knee.

A choke or chokehold is a general term for a constriction technique that is intended to prevent air or blood from passing through the neck to the brain. The lack of air or blood leads to unconsciousness. In some cases, the chokehold can lead to death.

The chokehold is considered a very effective finishing technique in martial arts and law enforcement. It is viewed as superior to brute-force manual strangulation, which requires a large disparity in physical strength to be effective.

There are two types of chokes—air chokes and blood chokes. Air chokes work by compressing the frontal airway (trachea and larynx), hence interfering with breathing and leading to asphyxia (suffocation).

Blood chokes, sometimes referred to as "sleeper holds," are a form of strangulation, and they work by compressing one or more of the carotid arteries (without compressing the frontal airway). The carotid arteries are major blood vessels in the neck that supply blood to the brain, neck, and face. There are two carotid arteries, one on the right and one on the left.

Blood chokes that target the carotid arteries can cause cerebral ischemia (insufficient blood flow to the brain), which leads to cerebral hypoxia (lack of oxygen). A powerful blood chokehold can cause unconsciousness in a matter of seconds (hence the term "sleeper hold"), and it requires very little physical strength.

A joint lock is a grappling technique involving manipulation of the opponent's joints in such a way that the joints reach their maximal degree of motion.

Joint locks cause pain by inflicting damage to critical joint tendons, cartilage, ligaments, and muscles. In most cases, a hyperextended joint will do the trick if you want to discourage the opponent and weaken his ability to continue the fight. When applied forcefully, power joint locks may cause joint dislocations or bone fractures.

Joint locks include arm locks, leg locks, small joint manipulation, spinal locks, ankle locks, and wristlocks.

Now you know that there is more to combat power than just knockout striking power. To become a *complete* power fighter, you must develop the ability to incapacitate opponents with *comprehensive* power-- through striking, throwing, choking, and locking.

Chapter 2

Combat PowerSync™

Applied Power

Viewing it from the most simplistic perspective—knockout power has two basic requirements:

1. That you *generate* enough force to "potentially" knockout or incapacitate your opponent.

2. That you *connect* with enough force to "actually" knockout or incapacitate your opponent.

Generating power is only *potential* power. Connecting with power is *applied* power!

Developing the ability to generate enough power for a knockout is a critical first step for the combat power student. However, simply *generating* power is not enough to finish the job. In order to actually deliver a knockout--you must be equally skilled in *connecting* with power.

Applied power (or connecting with power) is an advanced skill, and its mastery often separates advanced combat power students from beginning students or raw power fighters.

In my book, *Speed Training for Combat*--I discussed the differences between demonstration speed and applied speed. Many fighters have witnessed demonstrations of movement speed when an instructor throws blinding punches in the air. However, it is much more difficult to actually *apply* speed in a real fighting situation.

It is the same with power. You and I are much more concerned with developing the ability to apply power (and speed) in a real fighting situation, than we are with staged demonstrations of potential speed or power.

Flow Power

Flow power is the ability to connect with power repeatedly or during a combination of attacks. A fighter who has a knockout left hook, but couldn't hurt a fly with his right cross and kicks like a pigeon, does not possess flow power--although he can generate and connect with singular power (his signature left hook).

With flow power, you can truly overwhelm an opponent because you are able to deliver multiple power strikes, throws, and submissions in a fluid and relentless attack. It is very difficult for an opposing fighter to counter or overcome advanced flow power.

It's simply a matter of having so many knockout weapons--and the ability to deploy them in a coordinated attack so quickly--that your opponent has no answer for avoiding a knockout or submission.

Flow power (and Combat PowerSync) requires that you let go of rigid concepts and predictable fighting patterns. You must be able to adapt to the situation at hand and apply the appropriate power techniques based on what the circumstances require. In other words, don't continue to execute your favorite (or even most powerful) technique if the correct opening is not available. Instead, adapt instantly and deliver the right knockout weapon without thought.

Combat PowerSync Overview

Now you know the power equation--P=WxS (power = weight x speed). You have knowledge of the basic science behind knockouts and submissions. And, you understand the importance of applied power and flow power.

Now it's time to introduce you to an advanced power concept that represents the synthesis of all combat power elements—*Combat PowerSync*.

Your ultimate effectiveness in delivering knockout power in a real fight will be determined by your Combat PowerSync level--or more specifically—your *total combat power.* Because Combat PowerSync is so important—let's go further into it so that you can internalize the essence of the concept.

Combat PowerSync is defined as follows: *The coordinated development, integration, and culmination of all individual power attributes and skills leading to maximum total power for applied combat.*

The formal definition of synchronization is--*the coordination of events to operate a system in unison.* Systems operating with all their parts in synchronization are said to be *in sync* (in harmony).

Combat PowerSync fully recognizes and comprises every element of power fighting and power science. This includes (but is not limited to) speed, weight, kinetics, timing, distance, accuracy, targeting, techniques, ranges, punches, kicks, elbows, knees, throws, chokes, locks, strength, stamina, balance, mental focus, and emotional control.

Another way to grasp this concept is to think of Combat PowerSync as consisting of the following interconnected phases:

1. *Isolation* and *development* of individual power attributes and skills.

2. *Integration* of attributes and skills for improved combat power.

3. *Culmination* (honing) of total combat power to the maximum point where you can instinctively and consistently execute a variety of knockout power techniques in any fighting situation.

As a dedicated power student--you must focus on the mastery of Combat PowerSync (in concept and practice) if you want to fully develop your knockout capabilities, and avoid being a "simple" knockout artist with one go-to move that may or may not work depending on your opponent's fighting style and capabilities.

Combat power masters have advanced PowerSync— which enables them to deliver devastating power from multiple angles, with either hand, through a variety of numbing kicks, smashing elbows and knees, lights-out body slams, and (when the fight goes to the ground) painful submissions that *win fights quickly and decisively*!

You will achieve maximum total power through mastery of Combat PowerSync. And, the fundamental purpose of this book is to help you accelerate the progression of your Combat PowerSync.

Isolation Principle

Because the first phase of Combat PowerSync involves the development of your individual attributes and skills---we have to address the concept of isolation in combat training.

The isolation principle can be used to make rapid progress in all components of your Combat PowerSync, thereby helping you achieve maximum total power in the shortest possible time.

Using the isolation principle requires that you totally commit and involve yourself with "here and now." This is where your absolute power lies. Do not concern yourself with "there and then," which deals with false perceptions of effectiveness.

You should maintain this sense of purpose, in the present, throughout every phase of your training sessions. For combat power purposes, realize that five minutes of intense and focused power attribute training is more productive and beneficial to your Combat PowerSync than fifteen minutes of lackadaisical training.

Here are some additional tips on how to use the isolation principle in your training:

1. Begin by clearing your mind and reviewing the exact power attribute or component you will be training, prior to beginning any drill or exercise.

2. Concentrate intensely on developing that attribute by giving it your total, undivided attention.

3. Train when and where you will not be disturbed unless there is an emergency (and if training with partners, try to make sure they are equally as focused).

The more you can break down an attribute or skill in training, the more productive the training will be. That is another purpose of Combat PowerSync. It is a conceptual vehicle, through which you can effectively isolate the parts of the whole to make significant and rapid improvement on the sum total.

Total Combat Power Progression

There are five classifications of combat power development training. Understanding the purpose and natural progression of the following classifications will help focus and manage your workouts for faster results and improved Combat PowerSync.

Classifications of Combat Power Training

1. Solo Non-contact

2. Static Solo Contact

3. Dynamic Solo Contact

4. Dynamic Partner Contact

5. Dynamic Combat

Let's briefly review each training classification.

1. Solo Non-contact – Developing power using non-contact training drills is a starting point for power development. Typically, the combat power student will use this type of drill to practice new techniques and develop proper body mechanics for generating power (often starting out at slower speeds before progressing to faster movements).

An example of a solo non-contact power drill is shadow boxing. Solo non-contact drills are considered basic, but effective tools for developing power.

2. Static Solo Contact – From solo non-contact training, you will advance to static solo contact training, which allows you to experience full contact and start "feeling" your power (based on the feedback / reaction of the targeted tool). Examples include drills with contact equipment that provides limited movement, such as the heavy bag, punching dummy and grappling dummy.

3. Dynamic Solo Contact – The third classification of training in the progression of your knockout power is dynamic solo contact. These drills are more challenging than static solo contact drills because the target is more difficult to hit with full power.

In dynamic solo contact training, the target equipment reacts more aggressively based on the angle and force of your strikes. The double-end bag and reflex bag are two examples of dynamic solo contact training tools. In this type of training, your Combat PowerSync will evolve beyond simple power generation as you learn how to "connect" with power on a more elusive target.

4. Dynamic Partner Contact – The fourth classification of power progression training is characterized by active movement with a training partner. Examples of dynamic partner contact training include combination-focused power drills using focus mitts or striking shields.

5. Dynamic Combat – The fifth and most advanced classification in the progression of knockout power training is actual fighting. You (and a partner) can choose the level of contact and rules of engagement.

Dynamic combat drills can range from light contact single-style sparring to all-out mixed sparring with power strikes, throws, and submissions. Try to make sure your full-contact sparring is realistic and represents the conditions of a real fight.

If you choose to impose sport-specific restrictions (for example--no kicking in boxing), you will compromise the development of your total combat power. In addition to developing your Combat PowerSync, full contact sparring with very limited restrictions (and proper protective gear) will help prepare you for a real street fight. *In self-defense, there is only one critical rule to remember for survival---there are no rules!*

Chapter 3

Power Principles

There are seven foundational principles of combat power. Understanding these key principles will help you "crack the power code" and improve your critical combat knowledge.

Always remember--*knowledge is power*! Study and apply the seven power principles in your training--and you will see faster progress in the development of your knockout power. Let's briefly review each power principle.

Mental Focus

The ability to focus exclusively and deeply on the task at hand (knocking out your opponent) is critical to developing impressive striking and submission power. If you want to become a superior power fighter, you must train yourself to "turn on" this hyper-focused mental state instantly.

Advanced combat power students with high levels of PowerSync are able to tune out all distractions. It's as if they *become fully possessed by the fighting spirit* when they square off with an opponent.

The power of mental focus and concentration can help you achieve more knockouts—and help you avoid knockouts. Most below average fighters tend to have lapses in concentration during a fight. *Superior fighters are able maintain concentration for longer periods of time—and they exhibit higher levels of mental toughness.*

In your training sessions, you should practice harnessing and focusing your energy (and adrenaline) to generate maximum power. If you are not mentally focused on executing with maximum power, your strikes and submissions will be weaker and less effective. If you want to *be* a knockout fighter, you have to first *believe* that you are a knockout fighter!

Superior fighters are confident, and they strive to control the fight, both physically and mentally. You can use your eyes to improve focus, reduce reaction time, and control the opponent psychologically.

When you are facing an opponent from long distance--you should focus intensely on his eyes. As you begin to close the gap, you should switch your focus to his torso so that you can react to openings and attacks. Once you are in the clinching or grappling range, you should rely on sensitivity (tactile reflexes) to manipulate the opponent.

Relaxation

One of the biggest differences I've noticed between beginning combat students and advanced students or champions is the degree of tension in their bodies when they fight. Champion fighters are ultra-relaxed at all times (even when defending against a power attack). When on the offensive, advanced power fighters appear to fire punches and kicks like precision-guided missiles that explode on contact with an opponent.

Relaxed strikes and submissions are faster *and* more powerful. For maximum power, your mind must be focused intensely, but your body must be relaxed. When an inexperienced fighter strains and tenses unnecessarily, he is actually *less* powerful and typically ends up "pushing" his strikes vs. "blasting" his strikes for more forceful impact.

Relaxation in combat is a quality that must be learned through active contact training and experience. It is not enough to intellectually understand it. You must condition yourself to control the physiological effects of fear and adrenaline by instinctively converting excess muscular tension into relaxed energy and explosive power.

The best way to learn how to relax in combat situations is to focus on controlling your breathing and feeling the difference between "inefficient tension" and "ready-state relaxation" (your muscles are poised and ready to explode). Learn to develop a keen awareness of body tension during your training drills. In a short time, maintaining optimal tension in the muscles will become second nature.

Power Base

The following statement might not sit well with some rigid traditional stylists, but *"not all fighting positions or stances are created equal when you want to deliver knockout power."*

Some fighting stances are good-looking on the big screen (in movies), but do little to help you generate the force required to incapacitate an opponent in a real fight. When was the last time you saw an exotic or animal-based fighting stance in a championship MMA bout or local neighborhood bar fight?

To strike with knockout force--you must have a solid base (fighting position) upon which you can generate maximum force.

For example, let's consider upright punching or boxing. If a fighter's stance is very narrow and stiff—with feet touching, knees straight, and heels on the ground—he will not generate significant power because he is executing from a weak power base or foundation.

Knockout power punchers know that a solid yet flexible stance—with feet shoulder width apart, knees bent, and weight on the toes—provides a superior base for generating maximum punching force.

I'm not saying that you can't generate any power from a weak power base. Perhaps if your opponent is half your weight--you have naturally blazing speed--and your opponent sticks out his chin for a clean hit—you could possibly generate enough power for a knockout despite a weak power base.

However, Combat PowerSync is all about generating (and connecting) with *maximum* power. A stronger base facilitates knockout power. But, don't just take my word for it. Try it for yourself by hitting the heavy bag with a strong fighting position and weak fighting position. I guarantee you will feel the difference immediately.

While there may be plenty of weak fighting stances or positions, there is really no one perfect power fighting position. The optimal power base is situational dependent (due to variations in fighters, range, environment, positioning, and techniques).

The key to mastering the power base principle is active experimentation during training. Focus on becoming skilled at finding and maintaining the power base, as this will improve your Combat PowerSync and enable you to deliver knockout power at any time in a fight.

Movement Relativity

The fourth principle of power focuses on footwork and the relative movement of competing fighters at the precise moment of impact or engagement. In the case of a power strike—the precise moment of impact is when your strike successfully connects with the opponent.

Movement relativity for combat is the science of increasing total force at impact by leveraging your movement *and* the movement of your opponent. Maximum force, power, and damage can be achieved when your strikes are thrown at the moment you *and* your opponent are moving forward (toward each other).

Throwing power strikes while moving backwards, or away from your opponent, will dissipate power and lessen the impact. Not many boxers can knock out an opponent while moving backwards (unless the opponent is charging forward).

To deliver optimal power to the target, you need to propel your body in the direction of the strike--and time the strike so that your opponent is adding more energy (power) to your punch by unknowingly moving toward it. This split-second dynamic--when combined with effective execution of all power principles--will often lead to a spectacular single strike knockout.

Combat power masters are capable of delivering devastating power with strikes that travel a very short distance. Part of their secret is being able to perfectly time and "catch" the opponent moving toward the strike--thus multiplying the force and damage.

Imagine yourself in a fight, and the opponent initiates a wild haymaker punch. You instinctively (from your power base) relax and quickly launch a counter short hook punch that catches your opponent flush on the chin with full power. Knockout achieved. After your opponent rises from the ground, perhaps you will thank him for helping you win the fight by inadvertently "running into your left hook."

Check out the following video link. It provides a great example of movement relativity's impact on knockout power. The video features a fight between favored light heavyweight boxing champion Chad Dawson, and the underdog Adonis Stevenson. In the split-second before the knockout, you will see Dawson attempt to throw a right cross. In doing so, Dawson's head and body are moving forward—and this movement adds incremental force to Stevenson's precision power shot. Adonis Stevenson's emphatic first round knockout of Chad Dawson was selected (by many boxing experts) as the 2013 "Knockout of the Year."

http://goo.gl/U6gxHw

You can use solo equipment and partner training sessions to practice application of the movement relativity principle.

Kinetic Linking

Powerful punches are not the result of having "hand power," and powerful kicks don't come from simply having extraordinary "foot power."

Generating maximum power, as delivered through the hand--in a one-punch knockout, requires skilled coordination of the entire body. Similarly, a high level of full-body coordination can be seen in the major league baseball player who generates enough power to hit a baseball over 400 feet. You don't simply "wake up one day" with the ability to hit a baseball 400 feet—no matter how physically strong you are.

The scientific reality is that maximum raw human power requires *skilled full-body synchronization.* This subtle, yet critical principle and skill is called *kinetic linking.*

If your goal is to maximize your combat power--you absolutely must study, practice, and master kinetic linking.

The concept of the "kinetic chain" originated in 1875, when a mechanical engineer named Franz Reuleaux proposed that if a series of overlapping segments were connected via pin joints, these interlocking joints would create a system that would allow the movement of one joint to affect the movement of another joint within the *kinetic link.*

It takes energy to drive speed and acceleration. If we can increase the amount of energy driving our fist, we will increase the acceleration of our fist. To increase this energy, we need to make use of as many muscles (and as much weight) as possible.

We must put our entire body into our strikes— not just the nearest muscle group. More muscles =

more energy—and more energy = more acceleration. The critical question becomes--*How can I efficiently transfer maximum energy from many distant muscle groups to the striking point?* In order to make full use of the energy being generated, it has to travel to the striking point in a seamless chain reaction—thus the term *kinetic linking.*

A knockout right cross punch starts from the ground and works its way up. First, the legs engage by pushing up off the ground and leaning slightly forward. Next, the hips add power by torquing toward the target. The core, back, and chest follows this rotation toward the target as the shoulder prepares for the launch. The arm snaps out in a corkscrew motion utilizing the tricep, forearm, and wrist. The entire motion is smooth, fluid and engages multiple muscle groups.

Try this. If you stand still and just push your rear fist straight out, it does not move very fast. However, if you engage your core muscles by rotating your torso and shoulders toward the target just before extending your arm out—your fist moves much faster (as if it was shot out of a sling).

This is where kinetic linking becomes a skill— in the efficiency of energy transfer from muscle group to muscle group. The ending motion of one muscle group should be the starting motion of the next group. If one muscle group moves to soon (or too late), the kinetic chain loses energy on its way to the striking point.

Revisiting the right cross example—you will use your feet, calves, thighs, glutes, hips, abs, and back to drive the abrupt rotation of your shoulders. As soon as your right shoulder is pointing at the target, you will use the culminated energy to explode your arm and fist forward with maximum force (weight) and velocity (speed).

Again, what is the power equation? That's right—P=WxS. As a power principle, kinetic linking includes weight leveraging *and* speed acceleration.

You can start practicing kinetic linking by choosing one power strike. Once you are comfortable with the concept and the movement dynamics, you can progress to practice kinetic linking with a variety of strikes and throws.

Regardless of the chosen power weapon---you should begin with isolating the energy (movement) from the individual links (muscles) in the kinetic chain. Going back to the right cross example, you could start by only focusing on the powerful rotation of your shoulders and "launching" your fist.

As you become more comfortable with isolated kinetic linking for individual muscle groups— you can advance to practice full-body kinetic linking for various knockout power moves. Pay attention to the sensations in your hips, core, back, shoulder, and arm muscles. The rotation and the launch should be coordinated in one fluid and smooth motion.

The following is a link to a video on kinetic linking (for punching power). Check it out. It provides a demonstration and further explanation on kinetic linking for power generation. http://goo.gl/yyKCqA

Contact Point

The sixth power principle is all about efficiency— achieving maximum effect with minimum effort. The contact point principle is a simple, but important power booster.

Knowing precisely *where* to direct your power is an important part of developing your knockout and submission skills. A contact point is *a vulnerable target* on the opponent. Superior fighters will always direct their power weapons to the most effective contact points.

Striking or manipulating the opponent's most vulnerable body parts (with sufficient power) will make it easier to achieve a knockout or submission. For example, a powerful kick to the head is much more likely to result in a knockout than an equally powerful kick to the forearm. Similarly, a right cross punch to the chin is much more likely to drop your opponent than a right cross directed to his shoulder.

As a combat power student--you must learn the most vulnerable contact points on the body, and know which weapons to use when attacking specific contact points. Your goal is to utilize the most capable knockout tool--with the most force--and against the weakest and softest possible target, in order to deliver a quick and decisive win.

In Chapter 5--I will cover the most effective power weapons in more detail. For now—let's review the most effective knockout and submission targets.

Chin and Jaw

In boxing, the chin and jaw are the number one target. Power punches to the chin account for more knockouts than any other target. If you can generate and connect with maximum force on your opponent's exposed chin--you are almost guaranteed a knockout. In addition--it is fairly easy to fracture an opponent's jaw with a well-placed knockout punch to the chin.

A well-placed punch to the chin causes the head to suddenly spin around. After a fraction of a second, it quickly slows down as muscles, tendons, and bones prevent the head from spinning any further. The brain inside the skull is floating in fluid. It accelerates slower than the rest of the head. This forces it to crash into the inside of the skull when the head stops.

When the brain slams into the inside of the skull, it suffers trauma. It then bounces off the inside of the skull and slams into the opposite side. This causes even more trauma. Depending on the force of the punch, this can happen several times before the brain comes to a stop inside the skull.

The trauma to the brain stimulates an overwhelming number of neurotransmitters to fire at the same time. This essentially overloads the nervous system sending it into a state of temporary paralysis. The person who is hit in the jaw loses consciousness and his muscles relax. The injured person falls to the ground with no memory of being hit. This is the science of the one-punch knockout.

Ideal weapons for attacking the opponent's chin and jaw include the cross punch, hook punch, uppercut punch, elbows, and knees.

Neck and Throat

For submissions, the neck is a favorite target of power grapplers. Learning how to choke an opponent is a critical skill for success in mixed martial arts and street fighting.

For striking, the throat is an effective target for incapacitating an opponent. A fast, powerful strike to the throat can crush the opponent's larynx and cause the opponent to temporarily stop breathing. It is a very effective self-defense target because it doesn't require overwhelming force to stop an opponent.

Ideal weapons for attacking the neck include rear naked choke, triangle choke, guillotine choke, and neck crank. A cross punch is the most effective power weapon for attacking the throat. However, a throat strike can do significant damage to an opponent even with a less powerful weapon (such as the jab punch or knife hand strike).

Knee

The knee joint is designed to move in one direction only. A powerful strike to the knee can quickly incapacitate an opponent. The key is to focus on striking the knee so that it moves in an abnormal direction--which can result in a sprain, strain, tear, or dislocation.

The ideal weapons for attacking the knees during stand up fighting include power roundhouse kicks and side kicks. The weapons of choice for attacking the knees during grappling and ground fighting include knee bars and elbow strikes.

Elbow

The elbow joint is an excellent target for submissions during grappling and ground fighting. It is not a high interest target for power fighters during stand up fighting. Using an arm bar, you can quickly incapacitate an opponent—by causing tendon damage, fractures, or dislocations.

Groin

The groin is a very popular target for self-defense. Combat sports do not allow attacks to the unprotected groin. A powerful (and precise) kick, punch, knee, or elbow strike to the most sensitive areas of the groin can cause excruciating pain and immediate incapacitation.

Solar Plexus and Liver

The solar plexus is located between the breastbone and the belly button. The liver is located on the right side of the stomach—just behind the lower right area of your rib cage.

A power strike to the solar plexus can quickly drop an opponent and leave him gasping for air. The force of your strike can push vital organs into an unnatural position. In addition, the diaphragm spasms and is forced to expel air, hence the term "knocking the wind out of someone."

The ideal weapons for attacking the solar plexus include the round kick, side kick, power knees, and shovel hook punches. Using a power throw, it is possible to slam the opponent so hard, that it knocks the wind out of him.

A liver shot is a punch, kick, or knee strike to the right side of the ribcage that damages the liver. Blunt force to the liver can be excruciatingly painful, and an especially effective shot will incapacitate a person. A power strike shocks the liver--the largest gland organ and a center of blood circulation--and can cause breathlessness or unconsciousness.

A liver strike is usually made with the left hand, left knee, or left foot—with the most popular liver weapon being a left shovel hook during clinch fighting.

There are many more vital targets on the human body. In fact, pressure point fighting is an art that requires specialized focus and training in attacking vital targets. I suggest you check out *Vital Point Strikes* by Sang H. Kim to learn more.

For your combat power training—focus on how to attack the major contact points with multiple power weapons, and you will become a more effective knockout fighter.

Penetration

If you've read my book *Speed Training for Combat*, you know that I believe speed is a critical component of success in fighting. If you can't hit your opponent because you are too slow to react--or because you telegraph every attack (giving your opponent ample time to evade or counter)--you will have trouble achieving your goals of becoming a superior fighter and knockout expert.

However, some fighters rely too much on their speed and quickness. Strict reliance on speed might not be a bad thing if all combat fighting were like amateur boxing (complete with headgear and extra padded gloves)--where speed and accuracy are rewarded with points.

But, in a real street fight or a professional level MMA bout--not having respectable power (to complement your speed) will put a fighter at a serious disadvantage and limit his ability to control the ranges and outcome of the fight. A determined opponent or attacker will blast right through a fast, but light offense and force the fight to close distance striking, grappling, and ground fighting.

Advanced combat power students understand that a knockout requires commitment. By commitment, I really mean penetration power (or full power). Your strikes, throws, and submissions must *penetrate the contact point* in order to deliver maximum energy (power) and cause maximum displacement (damage). Naturally, this all-out commitment entails some element of risk---which comes in the form of a potential counter-attack from the opponent.

Despite the risk of counter-attack, power fighters do not focus on striking the surface of a target contact point. Instead, they are fixated on *smashing through the target* in order to knock the opponent down, out, or at least off balance. In a grappling situation, the power fighter's goal is to *push or pull through the contact point* in order to force the displacement that delivers a winning submission.

Most martial artists and people familiar with Bruce Lee's fighting system have probably seen the demonstration of his legendary inch punch. Bruce's objective was to show how a fighter could generate tremendous power from a very short distance.

Lee, holding his outstretched hand only one to six inches from a volunteer's chest, would explode with a punch that would hurl the volunteer backwards several feet into a waiting chair. Check out the video link below to see a demonstration.

http://goo.gl/UDtiHa

Bruce Lee's inch punch demonstration video provides an exaggerated example of the penetration power principle. The force generated by Lee comes from punching *through* the contact point (so much so that some would say it's more of a push than a punch).

Of course, in a real fight, the opponent will not stand squarely in front of you, waiting for a punch. However, I have found inch punch training to be very helpful in developing kinetic linking skills and penetration power.

Power Training Tip

My sequencing of the seven power principles outlined in this chapter was deliberate. You have studied each principle in the order that it comes into play during a combat power move. *Focus* your mind—*relax* your body—*stabilize* your position—*time* your movement—*launch* your weapon—*contact* the target—*penetrate* the target. This simple sequence represents the essence of the power principles in action!

I suggest you revisit this section occasionally, to refresh your knowledge of these foundational power principles. Often, I will gain new insights and clarity after rereading combat education material—particularly after I have had some time to apply the learnings in training and fighting.

Chapter 4

Power Attributes

Combat attributes are the characteristics or qualities of the individual fighter, without regard for their particular fighting style, system, or techniques. For example, power is an attribute—whereas, a Muay Thai round kick is a striking technique from a specific fighting system.

Due to advances in sports science and technology--and the proliferation of hybrid combat systems and cross-training---the latter part of the 20th century brought increased focus on the importance of attributes in combat sports.

Certain fighting attributes are genetically more prevalent in some fighters, but a committed and knowledgeable fighter (who embraces modern science and training tools) can significantly improve the functional level of all attributes.

Generally, no single fighting attribute trumps all others. Instead, it's the totality of the attributes when applied with skill and effective methods that will ultimately determine fighting competency.

The information in this guide is specifically designed to help you improve the attribute of power. Superior fighting power is a *primary attribute* that—unlike some attributes—is dependent on other attributes for its optimal development and application. These dependent attributes of power are highlighted in this chapter.

Balance

In the previous chapter, we discussed the fact that you must have a solid power base in order to generate intense power and force. Balance (in a power fighter) is the ability to *maintain* a solid power base while moving and adjusting in a real fight. Superior balance allows you to maintain your power base, which means that you are *always in a position to attack with power.*

The attribute of maintaining a power base in movement can be more accurately described as *dynamic balance.* It is active, fluid, and practical in its constant adaptation to the circumstances of the fight. Caution: This is not static balance—and has little to do with the ability to stand on one leg or hold a kicking position for an extended period of time.

Great footwork in a fighter is partially a manifestation of excellent balance. Fighters with exceptional balance and footwork have the ability to place themselves in the right place at the right time, which increases their odds of executing the right power techniques.

The key to dynamic balance is to develop your *kinesthetic perception* (sense of muscle movement) to the point where you know when your body is in position to execute with power and when it is not.

In combat, the advanced power fighter can go forward, backward, to the left, and to the right--from long range to medium range to close range--and from stand up to ground fighting—all without losing his power base.

Speed

Speed is directly related to power, as proven in the power equation ($P=W \times S$). A faster attack is a more powerful attack (assuming no difference in the weight of the attack). Simply put--*more speed equals more power!*

Beyond the benefit of increased velocity and power in your attacks--superior speed allows you to use the movement relativity principle to increase your power because your opponent is less likely to see a swift attack coming (and consequently, is more likely to be caught still or moving toward the impact).

You may have heard of a knocked out boxer later saying that he "never saw the punch coming."

A power strike that is invisible to the opponent (because it is quick and well-timed) has a high chance of delivering a knockout. On the contrary—a slow, looping, telegraphed power strike is usually very visible and allows the skilled opponent plenty of time to evade or counter.

Nearly all fighters are enamored with the idea of possessing blinding speed and cat-like reflexes. Indeed, speed is an essential attribute for fighting and self-defense. Regardless of your combat style or method—martial arts, boxing, wrestling, or MMA— you cannot apply it unless you can react quickly and respond accurately!

However, the vast majority of fighters do not fully understand the intricacies of how to maximize this highly touted attribute. Don't be seduced by spurious instructors who claim (or even demonstrate) that they can throw 20 punches in one second! You— the informed combat power student—know that such demonstrations have little, if anything, to do with *applied* speed and knockout power in full-contact competition and self-defense.

Superior combat speed requires more than just discernable movement speed. In reality, applied combat speed consists of seven interdependent components, known as the *Speed Loop™*. The Speed Loop is an advanced concept for speed training. It was designed to isolate, transform, maximize, and integrate the seven components of fighting speed.

You will use training tools (covered in Chapter 6) to develop your speed attributes. If you would like to learn more about the Speed Loop training system, I suggest you check out my book (and companion title) on *Speed Training for Combat*.

Speed Training Tip

The quickest and most effective way to improve your total combat speed is to frequently train with someone in whom these attributes function at a higher level than in yourself. In other words—you will get faster by training with someone who is faster than you!

Timing

One online dictionary defines timing as "the choice, judgment, or control of when something should be done." Timing in sports can be further defined as "selecting the best moment to do something in order to achieve the desired or maximum result."

Timing in combat is the ability to execute the right move at the right time in order to successfully attack (or defend against) an opponent. A fighter without good timing will be less successful in using his power or speed to win fights.

Timing is an advanced attribute, and it is often misunderstood or not appreciated by beginning combat fighters. Unlike power or speed, both of which are easily seen or demonstrated--timing is more subtle and not obvious to the untrained eye.

Combat power is generally viewed from the perspective of *dispatching* with force. Combat timing is specifically focused on *connecting* with force.

Smart power fighters do not underestimate the usefulness of the timing attribute--nor its influence on their ability to achieve knockouts.

Distance

Distance is the amount of space between two things. In Japanese martial arts, the term *Maai* translates simply to "interval," and refers to the space between two opponents in combat; or more formally, the "engagement distance."

The goal of Maai is the correct use of distance (or *distancing*). Distancing is the appropriate selection of distance between you and the opponent throughout an encounter. It applies to both unarmed and armed combat.

Distancing is an important concept in all combat sports and arts because it determines both offensive and defensive options for the combatants. Experienced fighters will often use distancing in conjunction with the attribute of timing in order to control the fight.

Although some styles of combat train practitioners in multiple ranges, most styles specialize in one or two ranges. Many fighters have their own unique expressions for various distances or ranges that are often derived from their preferred combat system.

Don't let your strength become your weakness. Superior power fighters are able to adapt instantaneously, and they can deliver knockout power from any distance or range! For maximizing Combat PowerSync, I advise fighters to *become competent in all ranges by cross-training in a variety of combat systems.*

Ask five different combat sport participants to name all of the ranges of combat, and you will most likely get five different lists. I know because I've asked dozens of people about combat ranges, and invariably--I end up smiling politely, scratching my head, and wondering if there is any way to make sense of it all!

To help clarify and simplify the interrelated concepts of distance and ranges in fighting, I have created the *Combat Range Matrix*™ (a matrix is simply an arrangement of connected things). However, before simplifying the combat ranges---I should introduce my theory of *distance perspective* and how it affects fighting distance and range.

When I ask someone to name the ranges of combat, I typically follow up by asking, "from whose perspective are the ranges defined?" This is a very important consideration. Without clarifying if the range is defined by the physical stature and stylistic paradigms of fighter A or B—we may end up with a skewed, incomplete, or unclear conclusion.

For example, when Bruce Lee fought Kareem Abdul Jabbar in *The Game of Death*, he used a variety of kicks to attack. Similarly, Kareem used a very effective front kick to knock Bruce down in the beginning of their fight scene.

Now, I ask--in both cases--were they in the kicking range? The answer? It depends on *distance perspective*. For Bruce--he was in kicking range during his offensive attack—and he was in non-contact range during Kareem's kicking attack. For Kareem— he was in kicking range during his offensive attack— and (due to his 7'2" height) he was in *punching* range during Bruce's kicking attack.

My distance perspective theory contends that *most fighters will define distance and range from their own perspective*. There is nothing inherently wrong with this. It's simply my hope that it helps to clarify the concepts of distance and range for you.

Now, let's get back to the combat range matrix. Combat range is really determined by two key factors—*position* and *activity*.

Below are the five combat positions.

1. Standing

2. Sitting

3. Squatting (or crouching)

4. Kneeling

5. Lying

Below are the five combat activities.

1. Non-contact

2. Kicking

3. Punching

4. Clinching (trapping; knees; elbows)

5. Grappling (takedowns; throws; submissions)

The following chart provides a snapshot of the Combat Range Matrix. The key thing to remember is this—*you can do any activity from any position.*

The numbers represent the combination of the activity and position. For example, the combat sport of boxing is concentrated in combat ranges 3 and 4 (standing punching and standing clinching)--whereas the combat sport of wrestling covers combat ranges 4, 5, 14, 15, 19, 20, 24, and 25.

5 x 5 Combat Range Matrix™

Position

	Non-contact	Kicking	Punching	Clinching	Grappling
Standing	1	2	3	4	5
Sitting	6	7	8	9	10
Squatting	11	12	13	14	15
Kneeling	16	17	18	19	20
Lying	21	22	23	24	25

Activity

©2014 by J. Barnes

The Combat Range Matrix is a framework that attempts to go beyond inadequate and outdated range labels, by clearly delineating *fighting situations.* By understanding every fighting position and activity combination---you can focus your distance training, and elevate your Combat PowerSync by isolating and improving the critical "power gaps" in your fighting game.

As a combat power fighter, your distance attribute training goals should include:

1. Develop proficiency in combat distancing (controlling the distance).

2. Develop reliable power weapons for *every* combat range (fighting situation).

Accuracy

Accurate attacks are precise and successful in connecting with the intended target. For the combat power fighter--accuracy is a critical attribute for achieving knockouts, submissions, and wins. Without accuracy--a fighter is not capable of delivering maximum force to the opponent's vulnerable targets.

An accurate athlete is a better athlete. For example, successfully batting a fast-pitch baseball requires outstanding accuracy. If the bat strikes the ball far from the center--it might strike the ball at an angle--forcing the ball to go straight up into the air, or bounce down into the ground. However, if the bat strikes the ball accurately at the center--the maximum force will be transferred---sending the ball the farthest distance in the intended direction.

Study the long-running champions in combat sports and you will find that they have high levels of the accuracy attribute. For example---Floyd Mayweather Jr. is one of this era's most masterful boxers. Sure—he has great defense. But, if you dig deeper into his boxing stats---you will find that Floyd's connect ratio (the critical measure of accuracy) is off the charts. He doesn't throw a lot of punches, but according to CompuBox™—he lands punches at the highest connect percentage (currently 42%) in the entire sport.

Accurate power fighters have the ability to connect forcefully with chosen targets over and over again (resulting in consistent knockouts and submissions). Unlike less-skilled power fighters, who may resort to swinging wildly like a child on the playground in his first scuffle--the advanced power fighter delivers attacks with lethal precision to the opponent's vulnerable body parts.

Improving your accuracy requires the development of coordination between your power weapons and your eyes. In Chapter 6, we'll cover specific tools and drills for developing pinpoint accuracy.

Strength

Physical strength is the ability to exert force on physical objects using muscles. For the purpose of developing knockout power—increased strength is vital for generating more velocity and greater penetration.

An individual's physical strength is determined by two factors--the cross-sectional area of muscle fibers recruited to generate force, and the intensity of the recruitment. The genetic inheritance of muscle fiber type sets the outermost boundaries of physical strength limits, though the achievement of maximum innate strength is determined by training (barring the use of enhancing agents such as testosterone).

For centuries--combat sport participants and observers have debated the role and relative value of strength for improving athletic performance. Up until the last few decades of the 20th century, many people falsely believed that intense strength training (and weight training in particular) was detrimental to the development of superior fighting skills for martial arts and boxing.

The myths surrounding strength and weight training have since been thoroughly debunked by scientists, trainers, coaches, and record-breaking athletes. We now know for sure—a stronger athlete is a better athlete!

Stronger muscles are faster muscles (despite the misguided old stereotypes of slow, muscle-bound bodybuilders). You can look to the world's elite sprinters to see that strength and muscular development are critical components of superior speed generation.

The ability to demonstrate high levels of speed in movement is closely related to the ability to contract and relax the muscles forcefully and quickly throughout movement and motion. You may have heard track and field announcers describe sprinters in the final few meters of a race as—*"powering through* to the finish line." This crucial moment in the race is when the sprinter maximizes the recruitment of "fast twitch" muscle fibers to reach peak acceleration as he crosses the finish line.

Similarly, in combat fighting, the ability to quickly contract and relax the muscles when striking will result in more speed. The ability to generate more force (due to superior strength) during a chokehold, throw, or joint lock will lead to more submission wins.

You can certainly train to develop knockout power without gaining Olympic-level powerlifting strength. However, *progressive weight training is necessary if you want to achieve your maximum combat power potential.*

Stamina

Stamina is the ability to sustain prolonged physical or mental effort. Physical stamina refers to the ability of the heart and lungs to function during higher-intensity activity. Your heart and lungs supply increased amounts of blood and oxygen to meet the demands of prolonged physical activity. This can also be referred to as cardiovascular endurance.

When your heart beats, blood is supplied to your body. With increased activity--your heartbeat and the amount of blood supplied to your body increases. With each breath--your lungs supply oxygen to your body. With increased activity, the number of breaths and the amount of oxygen supplied to your body increases.

Stamina level in sports is closely tied to the execution of skill and technique. A well-conditioned athlete can be defined as--the athlete who executes his technique consistently and effectively with the least effort.

In combat, stamina is the ability to continue fighting with maximum speed, power, and accuracy for a prolonged period of time. While the successful knockout fighter might not always need superior stamina--it has been proven that in most fights— stamina is a critical factor in determining the outcome and winner.

For any fighter—the loss of stamina has an immediate and adverse effect on all other attributes. Without stamina—power diminishes, speed declines, timing misfires, and strength dissipates.

Endurance training is the act of exercising to increase endurance or stamina. Combat endurance training can be divided into four categories including:

1. General aerobic endurance (low to moderate intensity; with continuous oxygen; 10 minutes or more; example--walking)

2. Specific aerobic endurance (low to moderate intensity; with continuous oxygen; 10 minutes or more; example--light shadow fighting)

3. General anaerobic endurance (high intensity; without continuous oxygen; less than 10 minutes; example--sprinting)

4. Specific anaerobic endurance (high intensity; without continuous oxygen; less than 10 minutes; example--full contact sparring)

A heart rate monitor is a device that measures and displays the heart rate in real time. This convenient fitness tool can help you improve your stamina by providing accurate feedback on the intensity and effectiveness of your endurance training--based on increases and decreases in your displayed heart rate.

You will notice the following physiological changes as your endurance, stamina, and fitness levels improve—your resting heart rate will decline (your stronger heart and lungs need less work to deliver the body's required amount of blood and oxygen)—your heart requires an increasingly higher level of intensity to reach your target exercise heart rate (your heart and lungs function more efficiently and with less stress at any given exercise intensity)—and your working heart rate will recover and decline from high intensity exercise faster (your stronger heart and lungs need less rest between bouts of anaerobic exercise).

By developing the superior stamina attribute—you will be capable of executing successful knockouts and submissions in later rounds or stages of a fight when your opponent is tiring. The ability to *maintain maximum power* for the duration of a tough fight against a skilled opponent will significantly elevate your Combat PowerSync proficiency.

Killer Instinct (KI)

As a serious combat power student, you must learn to control the natural rush of adrenaline that surges through your body during a fight. This is an essential skill for competition and self-defense.

Combat sport participants and enthusiasts often refer to this intense state of concentration and physical climax as a moment of "killer instinct"--when you are going for the winning strike, combination, throw, or submission. In this state--you are free from fear, anger, apprehension, and ego. You are simply in a programmed state of natural destruction!

Killer instinct can be described as a cold, detached, primal, and intense mentality that totally consumes your mind and transforms you into a vicious fighter. Simple knowledge of power principles and techniques will not create a superior fighter on the street or in the ring. To become a feared fighter who is capable of devastating power knockouts and submissions--you must learn to harness, sharpen, and manage the killer instinct mentality.

Ever notice how wide open a so-called maniac's eyes are when he flies into a rage? Well, emerging victorious from a violent attack on the streets might require you to become a maniac yourself. Your goal is to develop the same level of intensity, but yours will be a focused and controlled rage.

If necessary, you must develop the ability to switch instantly from a calm and rational human being into an unstoppable fighter who is determined to legally incapacitate a ferocious attacker at all costs! The thought of inflicting pain on a human may be brutal and uncomfortable, but it could save the lives of you and your family members. Having control of your killer instinct allows you to instantly cut off the adrenaline flow and avoid inflicting unnecessary harm or injury on your attacker or opponent.

In order to fully optimize your killer instinct, you must become very familiar with the adrenaline rush—that is sometimes referred to as the "fight or flight" response. I believe the control and use of the adrenaline rush is, in fact, the same inner power that is known in martial arts circles as Ki or Chi. Typically—the loser of a physical fight is the one whose adrenaline flow and killer instinct have been weakened. The truth is---effective fighting (at advanced levels) is more about controlling your mind and emotions than controlling your body.

High-functioning killer instinct will provide you with the following benefits in a fight.

1. Emotional Control – Killer instinct helps you override fear and fills you with unshakable confidence despite the situation or potential odds against you.

2. Mental Control – Killer instinct allows you to instantaneously take control of your mind and focus it like a laser on the singular objective of defeating an opponent (or group of opponents).

Killer instinct will expand your consciousness--and it supports very rapid, creative problem solving (heightened flow) to address and eliminate the threat (in the case of a self-defense situation).

3. Pain Control – Killer instinct allows you to temporarily block out pain in order to finish the task at hand (in this case—achieving a knockout or submission).

An additional benefit (or bonus) of fully functioning killer instinct is that it tends to have an adverse effect on your opponent. You will notice that when you fight opponents with lower levels of killer instinct—and less control of their adrenaline rush—you will be able to control the fight mentally and emotionally, which makes it easier for you to achieve a knockout or submission.

Highly developed killer instinct (backed up with superior skills) will allow you to "break down" your opponent's confidence and impose your will. Once you can do this, you are almost assured victory—because the body will always follow the mind (for better or worse).

The controllable components of killer instinct are breathing, mental focus, emotional control, and physical relaxation. It is not natural to have controlled breathing, sharp focus, and a relaxed body during a physical confrontation. Quite the contrary. Typically, untrained fighters will experience uncontrolled breathing, confusion, extreme stress, and heightened muscular tension during a fight.

When it comes to killer instinct—you must train yourself to do the unnatural. Superior fighters are comfortable in the realm of highly charged adrenaline rushes and physical fights. With proper knowledge and training--you will quickly *learn to activate and de-activate the killer instinct switch*!

To instantly turn your Ki or Killer Instinct on, try this: Open your eyes as wide as you can. Begin taking slow and deep breaths. Now relax and concentrate on the energy flowing through your body. Try to really feel the energy. It's just the oxygen that you're breathing in. It is oxygen that fuels the adrenal response.

Next, speed up your breathing as fast as you can, still breathing very deeply. Conjure up feelings of extreme fear or anger by using past experiences or unpleasant images. This causes electricity to surge through the brain and begins the adrenaline rush.

To instantly cut your Ki off, try this: Close your eyes. Slow your deep breathing. Relax your mind and body. Conjure up a feeling of peace and happiness. This will stop the adrenaline rush.

Practice cutting your killer instinct on and off during your training and sparring sessions.

Chapter 5

Strikes, Takedowns, Chokes, and Locks

To consistently win by knockout or submission--you must become highly skilled in utilizing *proven power techniques*. In this chapter--I will highlight the most effective power strikes, throws, takedowns, chokes, and locks. Outside of your current go-to power moves—and beyond the power weapons discussed in this chapter—I encourage you to develop an insatiable curiosity for new power techniques that can expand your knockout arsenal.

Not all fighting techniques are created equal when it comes to stopping power. The same goes for fighting styles. Your goal should be to identify and develop strikes, throws, and submissions that can incapacitate an opponent and win a fight with the least amount of effort and time.

Do not allow your potential to be hampered by limiting techniques, methods, or philosophies. You should always experiment with your power weapons in various combat ranges to ensure the development of striking and grappling effectiveness in all fighting situations—and the continuing evolution of your Combat PowerSync.

A recent scientific study has shown that *"people learning a new skill might pick it up more quickly by watching videos of other people performing the same task."* The study concluded that---*"people who viewed training videos experienced 11 times greater improvement in their motor skills than people not provided the videos."*

The training video study was co-authored by Dr. Paolo Preziosa and presented at the American Academy of Neurology. Apparently, (through MRI scans), the team of researchers were able to determine that training videos appeared to boost brain functions related to motor control and visual processing.

Based on this research--I have included links to more comprehensive and demonstrative videos for each power weapon (rather than simple, but less effective pictures or illustrations). Please watch the videos and use them as a starting point to learn the basic movement for each technique.

Strikes

The following strikes are considered the most powerful, effective, and dependable in delivering a knockout. You should incorporate all of these strikes into your power training program. By doing so, you will develop knockout striking power in multiple ranges and from multiple angles. I encourage you to investigate and test additional power strikes from a variety of combat systems.

Punches

A punch is a striking blow with a closed fist. Contact with the intended target is made with the knuckles. Punches offer the benefit of being the fastest type of striking.

For most fighters--punching is easier to learn, more familiar, and more versatile than other striking weapons. However, improper technique and inaccurate punches can do more harm to the striker than the intended target (particularly in bare fisted street fights). You should learn how to make a proper fist and use good form when practicing the following knockout punches.

Cross (Straight) Punch

Combat Style: Boxing

Activity Range: Punching

Position Range: Standing; Sitting; Squatting; Kneeling

Power Source: Acceleration; Body Rotation; Rear Leg Push

Knockout Target: Jaw; Chin; Temple; Throat; Solar Plexus; Groin

Technique Summary: From the on guard position, the rear hand is thrown from the chin, crossing the body and travelling towards the target in a straight line. The rear shoulder is thrust forward and finishes just touching the outside of the chin. For additional power, the hips and torso are rotated as the cross is thrown. Weight is also transferred from the rear foot to the lead foot, resulting in the rear heel turning outward and pivoting.

Example: http://goo.gl/ylYE3x

Hook Punch

Combat Style: Boxing

Activity Range: Punching; Clinching

Position Range: Standing; Sitting; Squatting; Kneeling

Power Source: Body Rotation; Leg Push (lead or rear)

Knockout Target: Chin; Jaw; Temple

Technique Summary: From the on guard position, swing the lead arm (which is bent at an angle near or at 90 degrees) and hand in a horizontal arc toward the target. The hips, torso, and lead shoulder are rotated as the hook is thrown. Weight is also transferred from the lead foot to the rear foot, resulting in the lead heel turning outward. Pivoting on the lead foot increases the power of the hook punch. Hook punches can be thrown by either the lead hand or the rear hand (reverse the rotation direction for the rear hand hook).

Example: http://goo.gl/tjQEks

Uppercut Punch

Combat Style: Boxing

Activity Range: Clinching

Position Range: Standing; Sitting; Squatting; Kneeling

Power Source: Body Rotation; Leg Push (lead or rear)

Knockout Target: Chin; Jaw; Nose

Technique Summary: The punch moves as its name implies--it initiates from the lower torso and makes an upward motion before landing on the target.

The fist is raised vertically to strike the target. Since most on guard positions are held with the arms in a vertical position, the uppercut can be used to avoid the opponent's attempts at blocking. Uppercut punches can be thrown by the lead hand or rear hand.

Example: http://goo.gl/zjRuz9

Overhand Punch

Combat Style: Boxing

Activity Range: Punching

Position Range: Standing; Sitting; Squatting; Kneeling

Power Source: Acceleration; Body Rotation; Rear Leg Push

Knockout Target: Jaw; Chin; Temple

Technique Summary: From the on guard position, the rear hand is thrown in a semi-circular and vertical (top-down) punch toward the target. The rear shoulder is thrust forward and finishes just touching the outside of the chin. For additional power, the hips and torso are rotated as the overhand is thrown. Weight is also transferred from the rear foot to the lead foot, resulting in the rear heel turning outward and pivoting.

Example: http://goo.gl/AwPLhK

Shovel Hook Punch

Combat Style: Boxing

Activity Range: Clinching

Position Range: Standing; Sitting; Squatting; Kneeling

Power Source: Body Rotation; Leg Push (lead or rear)

Knockout Target: Solar plexus; Liver; Rib cage; Kidney; Heart; Groin

Technique Summary: A shovel hook is a power body punch that combines characteristics of both the uppercut and the hook. The punch moves somewhat as its name implies--it initiates from the lower torso and makes an upward inward motion before landing on the target. Shovel hook punches can be thrown by the lead hand or rear hand.

Example: http://goo.gl/1UkEiU

Kicks

Striking with your foot or leg has several advantages. First--your leg is much more powerful than your arm. Based on scientific measurement of force generation—kicking is the most powerful and damaging blow you can administer. Second--your leg is longer than your arm, so it is your first line of attack, normally preceding your punch. Third--blocking a powerful kick is difficult, especially on the low line areas like the shin, knee, and groin.

Unfortunately, too many martial artists do not derive maximum benefit from kicking, because they have not mastered the most effective knockout power kicks. Purely snapping or flicking kicks do not generate enough power to seriously hurt an opponent because they do not take full advantage of the scientific principles of power. The following kicks will deliver maximum force and proven knockout power.

Rear Leg Roundhouse Kick

Combat Style: Muay Thai; Tae Kwon Do; Capoeira

Activity Range: Kicking; Punching

Position Range: Standing; Sitting; Squatting; Lying

Power Source: Body Rotation; Weight Transfer

Knockout Target: Head; Neck; Torso

Technique Summary: Execution of the powerful rear leg roundhouse kick varies by combat style. In general, the kicker swings their leg sideways in a circular motion, kicking the opponent's side with the front of the leg--usually with the shin or instep.

The fighter delivering the roundhouse kick will also raise up on the ball of his non-kicking foot, mainly to allow for greater pivoting speed, and increased power. The hips are rotated into the kick in order to convey more force in the kick, and the abdominal muscles are strongly recruited in the act of rotation. Instead of simply snapping the kick, the combined action of the leg and hips creates a kick that is much more devoted to its momentum.

Muay Thai roundhouse kicks use the shin to make contact with the target instead of the instep. This adds to the structure of the kick, as the shin is more durable than the foot. Using the shin reduces the kick's reach, but allows it to be thrown within punching range. Capoeira uses the arms, in addition to the non-kicking leg, to help transfer more weight and force to the kicking leg.

Example: http://goo.gl/1Yp6vQ

Example: http://goo.gl/6NukoH

Side Kick

Combat Style: Jeet Kune Do

Activity Range: Kicking

Position Range: Standing; Sitting; Lying

Power Source: Acceleration; Body Rotation; Leg Extension

Knockout Target: Head; Neck; Torso

Technique Summary: The side kick refers to a kick that is delivered sideways in relation to the body of the person kicking. More traditional styles of martial arts utilize whipping or snapping of the knee to generate power in the side kick. The JKD adaptation of the side kick can generate tremendous power and deliver force that can knock down or knock out an opponent.

The power of this kick is generated from momentum of the body moving toward the opponent quickly along with the twisting of the hips on impact. As with the Muay Thai roundhouse kick--the key to the JKD side kick's power is to utilize as much weight as possible to inflict maximum damage on the opponent. There are two areas that are commonly used as impact points in a side kick--the heel of the foot or the outer edge of the foot. The heel is more effective for power kicking.

Example: http://goo.gl/Ob9IxM

Example: http://goo.gl/IhyXHK

Spinning Back (Hook) Kick

Combat Style: Tae Kwon Do; Capoeira

Activity Range: Kicking

Position Range: Standing

Power Source: Body Rotation; Acceleration

Knockout Target: Head; Neck; Solar Plexus

Technique Summary: From the on guard position, the fighter spins 180 degrees, pivoting on the non-kicking foot. As the spin begins--the fighter quickly turns his head to look over his shoulder before launching the hook kick and striking the side of the opponent. This kick traditionally uses the heel to strike with. The force in this kick is generated by extreme rotation. With that said, this kick can be somewhat difficult and potentially dangerous to pull off in competition or a real fight. Nevertheless, make no mistake--if it is executed properly and connects--it has the capability and force necessary to knock out an opponent. Many MMA fights have ended with a well-placed spinning hook kick.

In Capoeira, the spinning back or hook kick (called Meia Lua de Compasso) is called the "king of kicks." The power of the Capoeira spinning back kick derives its energy from the same motion as the swing of a golf club or baseball bat. The transfer of power begins with a body spin and the hand slamming into the ground---and ends with the spin of the kicking leg and heel.

Example: http://goo.gl/xMtZR1

Example: http://goo.gl/T31AEq

Front Push (Stomp) Kick

Combat Style: Tae Kwon Do; Krav Maga; Muay Thai

Activity Range: Kicking

Position Range: Standing; Sitting; Lying

Power Source: Hip Thrust; Leg Extension

Knockout Target: Torso; Solar Plexus; Groin; Face

Technique Summary: The front push kick involves raising the knee and foot of the striking leg to the desired height and extending the leg to contact the heel of the foot with the target. Thrusting the hips is a common method of increasing power of the kick. When standing, the kick is typically executed with the upper body straight and balanced. The stomp kick employs the same mechanics as the push kick. Stomp kicks can be executed from a standing position (kicking downward) or lying position (kicking straight out or upward). Stomp kicks are versatile--they can be used against a lying opponent when you are standing—and against a standing opponent when you are lying down.

Example: http://goo.gl/LIU6bD

Example: http://goo.gl/hspFuM

Elbows

The elbow strike is one of the most devastating strikes you can use in close quarters combat and self-defense. It is a strike with the point of the elbow, the part of the forearm nearest to the elbow, or the part of the upper arm nearest to the elbow. The hardness of the elbow allows for hitting with considerable force--and capable fighters can easily knock out, cut, or injure their opponent with a well-placed elbow strike.

Hook Elbow Strike; Back Elbow Strike

Combat Style: Muay Thai

Activity Range: Clinching; Grappling

Position Range: Standing; Sitting; Squatting; Kneeling; Lying

Power Source: Body Rotation; Hard Striking Surface

Knockout Target: Chin; Jaw; Face; Solar Plexus; Groin

Technique Summary: Elbows can be thrown horizontally (similar to a hook punch) or vertically (similar to an uppercut) using the forearm--and backward (similar to a back kick) or downward (similar to a stomp kick) using the point of the elbow. The most powerful elbows for delivering knockouts or knockdowns are the hook elbow and back elbow strikes because they allow the fighter to generate more power through body rotation.

Elbows can be used in combination with punches or kicks to help close the distance. In addition—elbows are used in mixed martial arts as part of the "ground-and-pound" fighting tactic. Participants often use elbow strikes in conjunction with punches while in the full guard, half guard, side mount, or full mount in order to knock out or overwhelm the opponent.

Example: http://goo.gl/shKCh0

Example: http://goo.gl/xlI8vm

Knees

A knee is a strike with either the kneecap or the surrounding area. Kneeing is a disallowed practice in some combat sports, especially to the head of a downed opponent. Styles such as Muay Thai and several mixed martial arts organizations allow kneeing depending on the positioning of the fighters. The knee strike is a commonly used power weapon in self-defense and reality-based martial arts.

Straight Knee Strike

Combat Style: Muay Thai

Activity Range: Clinching; Grappling

Position Range: Standing; Sitting; Kneeling; Lying

Power Source: Hip Thrust; Hard Striking Surface

Knockout Target: Chin; Face; Solar Plexus; Groin

Technique Summary: The straight knee is the most common—and most powerful knee strike. It involves thrusting the front of the knee into the head, body, or groin of an opponent. A particularly effective clinching position for throwing straight knee strikes is the double collar tie, where the head of the opponent is controlled and pulled toward the knee strike to provide increased power. On the ground, straight knees can be effective from a few top positions such as the side control (side mount) and north-south position.

Example: http://goo.gl/VVrp68

Headbutts

A headbutt is a strike with the head, typically using the robust parts of the cranium as the area of impact. Effective headbutting involves using the forehead to strike a sensitive area on the opponent, such as the face or nose. It can be considered a very effective but risky maneuver as a misplaced strike can cause greater injury to the person delivering the headbutt than to the person receiving it.

Front Headbutt; Back Headbutt

Combat Style: Krav Maga

Activity Range: Clinching; Grappling

Position Range: Standing; Sitting; Squatting; Kneeling; Lying

Power Source: Neck Thrust; Torso Thrust

Knockout Target: Face

Technique Summary: Headbutts are best used from close range, such as from the clinch and on the ground. Parts of the cranium with thick bone and high local curvature make good weapon areas—including the forehead near the hairline, the back of the head, and the top of the head.

An effective headbutt can be performed with a forward, rising, sideways or backwards motion. The most effective and realistic headbutts for knocking out an opponent are the forward and backward headbutt—because they allow a fighter to generate more explosive force and thrust from the torso.

Example: http://goo.gl/0Nng0A

Example: http://goo.gl/w09Bgw

Throws and Takedowns

In the past, throws were most commonly associated with judo and takedowns with wrestling. However, with the growing popularity of martial arts and the rise of MMA--throws and takedowns have become synonymous with most martial-arts-based combat sports.

For the combat power fighter--throws and takedowns can setup knockout strikes or incapacitating submissions. However, a skilled power grappler can sometimes execute throws that end up in a knockout without requiring any follow-up strikes or submissions (particularly in a self-defense or street fighting situation).

A takedown is a technique that involves off-balancing an opponent and bringing him to the ground, typically with the fighter performing the takedown landing on top. The process of quickly advancing on an opponent and attempting a takedown is known as "shooting." Takedowns are usually distinguished from throws by the forward motion and targeting of the legs.

Combat throws involve off-balancing or lifting an opponent to throw him to the ground. Typically, the fighter performing the throw remains on his feet—however, he may sometimes end up on the ground in a top position if he does not disengage from the opponent.

The following throws and takedowns are generally considered the most powerful and effective in helping you setup or deliver a knockout or submission. You should incorporate all of these throws and takedowns into your power training program. I have not included many well-known (but less powerful) throws and takedowns, because I wanted to focus on the essential power throws and takedowns for strengthening your Combat PowerSync. However, I encourage you to check out a variety of grappling-based combat systems to learn more about power throws and takedowns.

Shoulder Throw

Combat Style: Judo

Activity Range: Grappling; Clinching

Position Range: Standing; Sitting; Squatting; Kneeling

Power Source: Body Rotation; Legs

Knockout Target: Head; Neck; Back; Shoulder

Technique Summary: The shoulder throw is the most popular throw in Judo. A shoulder throw involves throwing an opponent over the shoulder. The fighter grabs and pulls one of the opponent's arms with both hands—and simultaneously turns his back toward the opponent. Using his legs and hips for support—the fighter quickly lifts the opponent off the ground (and onto his back) and throws him over his shoulder and to the floor.

Example: http://goo.gl/9xAhw1

Example: http://goo.gl/Jz0sxx

Hip Throw

Combat Style: Judo; Wrestling

Activity Range: Grappling; Clinching

Position Range: Standing

Power Source: Body Rotation; Leg Extension

Knockout Target: Head; Neck; Back; Shoulder

Technique Summary: A hip throw involves using the thrower's hip as a pivot point. The fighter places his hip in a lower position than the opponent's center of gravity. The fighter pulls his opponent toward him as he turns his body, hoisting his opponent onto his hip and throwing him to the ground.

Example: http://goo.gl/K2PsZN

Example: http://goo.gl/Z8SHmf

Pick Up Throw

Combat Style: Wrestling; Judo

Activity Range: Grappling; Clinching

Position Range: Standing; Sitting; Squatting; Kneeling

Power Source: Body Rotation; Leg Extension

Knockout Target: Head; Neck; Back; Shoulder

Technique Summary: A pick up throw involves lifting the opponent off the ground and then bringing him down with a forceful slam to the ground. Common pick up throws are lifting variations of the double leg takedown, judo's *te guruma* or *sukui nage*, and the suplex from wrestling--in which the fighter lifts his opponent's body vertically and throws the opponent over his own center of gravity while executing a back fall (usually accompanied by a back arch).

Example: http://goo.gl/ZDea3t

Example: http://goo.gl/XkraZG

Example: http://goo.gl/4OQZ9n

Double Leg Takedown; Blast Double Leg Takedown

Combat Style: Wrestling; Judo

Activity Range: Grappling; Clinching

Position Range: Standing; Sitting; Squatting; Kneeling

Power Source: Acceleration; Leg Extension

Knockout Target: Head; Back; Shoulder; Solar Plexus

Technique Summary: In Judo, the double leg takedown is referred to as *morote*-gari. To perform a double leg takedown--the fighter grabs the opponent with both arms around the opponent's legs while keeping his chest close to the opponent. The fighter then uses his position, arms, and momentum to force the opponent to the ground. The fighter should be careful to avoid a counter strike or guillotine choke when executing a double leg takedown.

A more powerful variation of the traditional double leg takedown is the *blast double,* which is one of the most powerful and physically dominating takedowns in freestyle wrestling. Sometimes known as a "drive double" or "driving leg tackle," this effective leg attack closely resembles a "tackle" in American football. Although the blast double is a basic technique, its value is immense. If you practice this technique until you have the timing and the explosive power mastered, you will find that it becomes a go-to power move during grappling or clinching.

The target for the blast double leg takedown is the opponent's mid-torso. The fighter starts by making sure he is lower than the opponent. From there--the fighter explodes and takes a fast, deep step forward so that his lead foot lands between the opponent's feet. As he blasts (hits) the opponent in the midsection with his head and shoulders—the fighter grabs the back of his opponent's knees with both hands and pulls the opponent's legs as he drives through the takedown.

Example: http://goo.gl/MYEBDN

Example: http://goo.gl/euFqNc

Example: http://goo.gl/AafuCq

Submissions

A submission (also referred to as a "tap out" or "tapping out") is a combat sports term for yielding to the opponent, and therefore resulting in an immediate defeat. A submission is a grappling hold that is applied with the purpose of forcing an opponent to submit out of either extreme pain or fear of injury.

There are generally two types of submission holds: those that would potentially strangle or suffocate an opponent (chokes); and those that would potentially cause injury to a joint or other body part (locks).

Chokes are generally divided into two major categories—air chokes and blood chokes.

An air choke is a "true" choke that compresses the upper airway, interferes with breathing, and can lead to suffocation. A properly applied air choke will cause an opponent to submit very quickly because it causes excruciating pain and severe panic.

Blood chokes (also known as *sleeper holds*) are a form of strangulation that compress one or both carotid arteries and/or the jugular veins without compressing the airway. A well-applied blood choke may lead to unconsciousness in a matter of seconds. Compared to strangulation with the hands, properly applied blood chokes require little physical strength.

A joint lock is a grappling technique involving manipulation of an opponent's joints in such a way that the joints reach or exceed their maximal degree of motion. If applied forcefully, joint locks may cause severe injury to ligaments, muscles, and tendons—and even joint dislocations and bone fractures.

The following submissions are the most effective techniques for incapacitating an opponent. You should incorporate all of these power submissions into your training program. Of course--I encourage you to check out more power submissions by studying grappling-based combat systems.

Warning: Please use extreme caution when practicing chokes and joint locks in training. Careless use of these submission techniques may cause unintended injury to you or your training partners.

Rear Naked Choke

Combat Style: Brazilian Jiu-Jitsu

Activity Range: Grappling

Position Range: Standing; Sitting; Squatting; Kneeling; Lying

Power Source: Forearms; Biceps; Triceps

Knockout Target: Neck (Carotid Arteries-Blood Choke; Trachea-Air Choke)

Technique Summary: A simple and effective chokehold—the rear naked choke is the most common finishing hold in mixed martial arts competition. It is applied from behind the opponent and constricts blood flow from the carotid arteries to the brain. The fighter starts by looping one arm around the opponent's neck so that the crook of the elbow is under the opponent's chin—and the fighter places the hand of that arm on the opposite bicep. The other hand is then placed on the back of the opponent's head to push the head and neck forward into the crook of the flexed arm. Additional pressure may be applied by immobilizing the opponent's lower body--by locking the legs around the opponent's waist (referred to as "hooks") and arching the back to place more force against the neck.

Example: http://goo.gl/kFJor5

Example: http://goo.gl/Gu5Ke0

Example: http://goo.gl/w4rAzP

Triangle Choke (Arms Triangle; Leg Triangle)

Combat Style: Brazilian Jiu-Jitsu

Activity Range: Grappling

Position Range: Standing; Sitting; Squatting; Kneeling; Lying

Power Source: Forearms; Biceps; Inner Thighs; Hamstrings

Knockout Target: Neck (Carotid Arteries-Blood Choke)

Technique Summary: Another common finishing hold in mixed martial arts. A triangle choke is a "figure-four" chokehold, which strangles the opponent by encircling the opponent's neck and one arm with the legs (or arms) in a configuration similar to the shape of a triangle. The technique constricts the blood flow from the carotid arteries to the brain. Tactically speaking, the triangle choke is a very effective counter move from the bottom position, generally applied from the guard, or open guard (defensive positions). The need for isolation of one arm could be a rationale for the frequency with which this technique is attempted in combat sports--due to the brief vulnerability of one arm when executing hand strikes.

Example: http://goo.gl/Hx0DXa

Example: http://goo.gl/ru7tty

Example: http://goo.gl/DL3QEq

Guillotine Choke

Combat Style: Brazilian Jiu-Jitsu

Activity Range: Grappling

Position Range: Standing; Sitting; Squatting; Kneeling; Lying

Power Source: Forearms; Biceps

Knockout Target: Neck (Carotid Arteries-Blood Choke, Trachea-Air Choke)

Technique Summary: The guillotine choke is a chokehold applied from in front of the opponent. It is a common choke in mixed martial arts competitions and street fights. The choke involves using the arms to encircle the opponent's neck in a fashion similar to a guillotine. The arm is wrapped around the trachea, and the hands are clasped. Pressure is applied upwards. The technique is either a type of suffocation (air choke) that prevents airflow to the lungs--or a type of strangulation (blood choke) that restricts blood flow to the brain.

Example: http://goo.gl/unNIKs

Neck Crank (Can Opener)

Combat Style: Brazilian Jiu-Jitsu; Judo

Activity Range: Grappling

Position Range: Standing; Sitting; Squatting; Kneeling; Lying

Power Source: Forearms; Biceps; Triceps

Knockout Target: Neck; Spine

Technique Summary: A neck crank applies pressure to the neck by pulling or twisting the head beyond its normal range of rotation. It is technically a type of spinal lock.

Example: http://goo.gl/r6UJK5

Example: http://goo.gl/tS3UDG

Example: http://goo.gl/ZrKpdO

Arm Bar

Combat Style: Brazilian Jiu-Jitsu; Judo

Activity Range: Grappling

Position Range: Lying

Power Source: Body Rotation; Inner Thighs; Hamstrings; Forearms; Biceps

Knockout Target: Elbow Joint

Technique Summary: In general, the fighter secures one of the opponent's arms at the wrist, trapping it between his legs by squeezing his knees together. The fighter's legs end up across the opponent's chest, with the trapped arm held between the thighs, and the elbow pointing against the thigh or hips. By holding the opponent's wrist to his chest, the fighter can easily extend the opponent's arm and hyperextend the elbow. The fighter can further increase the pressure on the elbow joint by arching his hips against the elbow.

Example: http://goo.gl/WYzB4i

Example: http://goo.gl/hP0HAK

Example: http://goo.gl/q3CKXN

Knee Bar

Combat Style: Brazilian Jiu-Jitsu; Judo

Activity Range: Grappling

Position Range: Lying

Power Source: Body Rotation; Inner Thighs; Hamstrings; Forearms; Biceps

Knockout Target: Knee Joint

Technique Summary: A knee bar is a leg lock that can hyperextend the knee. The basic knee bar technique is similar to that of an arm bar. The fighter will trap the opponent's leg between his legs and secure the opponent's ankle with his arms--so the opponent's kneecap points towards the fighter's body. The fighter then applies pressure with his hips--forcing the opponent's leg to straighten and to hyperextend the knee joint.

Example: http://goo.gl/iZ7cRk

Example: http://goo.gl/lzkwLl

Power Training Tip

For combat power masters (regardless of their style or system)—connecting power weapons to vulnerable targets is the most simple and reliable strategy for achieving wins by knockout or submission. As a combat power student—you will progress more rapidly if you *focus your training on mastering the skill of attacking sensitive targets with proven power techniques.*

Chapter 6

Power Training Tools

Modern training tools have become a game-changer in the development of superior skills and attributes for all sports. Advances in training science and equipment have created faster, stronger, and more powerful athletes.

Many combat fighters (and athletes in general) were influenced by the legendary Bruce Lee. He is generally recognized as one of the founding fathers of mixed martial arts. In addition, Lee was well ahead of his time in terms of using equipment to maximize his fighting attributes.

Although he was not a large man, Lee was able to generate astounding power in his punches and kicks. Many of his training partners have provided first-hand accounts of being knocked down by Lee with a variety of strikes from straight jabs to crushing side kicks. One of the most valuable tools in Lee's equipment arsenal was the heavy bag. Bruce Lee developed enough explosiveness in his side kick to move a 100-pound heavy bag from a vertical hanging position to a fully horizontal position (and often caused the heavy bag to smack the ceiling due to the power behind his kick).

You *must* take full advantage of training equipment in order to maximize your combat power. The tools covered in this chapter will develop and hone your ability to generate power *and* connect with power. As you start to see and feel the progression of your power from consistent tool training--you will start to gain greater motivation, focus, and self-confidence. This creates a "cycle of success" that will ultimately lead to you becoming a more formidable fighter.

Given the importance of training equipment to your power development, you will need to get convenient access to quality tools. You can join a local boxing or MMA training gym. Or, you can purchase training tools through online retailers. If you can't afford to buy all of the tools, start with one or two and save up to purchase more tools later. Also, you can search popular online resell sites to find great deals on pre-owned training equipment.

Now, let's get into the specific training tools, equipment, and drills that will help you accelerate and maximize your knockout and submission power.

Power Breathing

There are four key benefits of proper and effective breathing during combat.

1. Relaxation (improves speed)

2. Focus (improves kinetic linking)

3. Penetration (improves contact power)

4. Stamina (delays muscle fatigue)

Without effective breathing techniques—you will not be able to optimize your fighting skills and Combat PowerSync. The following breathing exercises should be incorporated into your training.

Power Breathing Exercises

Start by practicing *slow power breathing*. You can practice *fast power breathing* after you are comfortable with power breathing at a slower pace. The most common breathing mistake made by beginning combat students is to breathe from the chest. For proper and effective breathing--you must train yourself to breath from the stomach.

Start by sitting or standing in a comfortable position. Focus on your breathing by pulling air into your stomach. As the air fills your lungs—your stomach should expand first, and then your chest expands. The expansion of your torso moves from the bottom (lower abdomen) to the top (upper chest). Initially, you may want to perform this exercise in front of a mirror so that you can see the torso movement, and make sure you are breathing properly.

Slowly breathe in and out--while mentally counting 5 seconds with each inhalation and 5 seconds with each exhalation. Repeat for 5-10 total cycles. Be sure to keep your body as relaxed as possible. If it helps you relax--you can close your eyes during this exercise.

Proficiency in slow power breathing will improve your relaxation, focus, and stamina. Once you are comfortable with slow power breathing from a resting position—you should progress to practice slow power breathing from your fighting position and (later) during training drills.

For fast power breathing—you will need to speed up the pace of the breathing—but you must continue to breathe fully and deeply. From a fighting position---start to quickly (and fully) breathe in and out. Each inhalation should only take 1 second. Each exhalation should only take 1 second. Repeat for 5-10 total cycles. Be sure to keep your body as relaxed as possible. As with slow power breathing---you can practice fast power breathing in front of a mirror to ensure correct technique.

Power fighters routinely exhale quickly and forcefully when executing their power moves. This provides increased kinetic linking and penetration power. For more advanced fast power breathing exercises—practice coordinating power strikes (and combinations of strikes) with quick, forceful exhalations.

Mastery of fast power breathing will improve your ability to maintain focus and power in the midst of an intense fight or bout.

Once you are comfortable with the basics of power breathing--you should start using power breathing during shadow fighting, equipment training, and sparring sessions. Focus on training yourself to automatically initiate and maintain power breathing during drills. When sparring—use fast power breathing during engagement—and slow power breathing during breaks or rest periods to help recover more quickly.

A longstanding myth related to proper combat breathing is that a fighter must breathe through the nose for best results. There is no scientific proof or basis for this assertion. The reality is that it doesn't matter if you breathe through your nose or mouth--as long as you breathe fully and deeply.

You can effectively relax, focus, maintain stamina, and generate knockout power when breathing through your mouth. However, I strongly encourage you to develop the habit of keeping your teeth clenched when fighting (this applies to mouth *and* nose breathers). Keeping your mouth wide open leaves you more vulnerable for a knockout (if your opponent connects with a strike to your jaw or chin).

Power Torquing

The following drills will help develop your kinetic linking skills and ability to "torque" more forcefully-- thereby putting more weight (and thus power) into your strikes and takedowns.

Hip Torquing Drill

Stand with your feet parallel as if you are in a face-off with an opponent before the fight or bout begins. Do not put one foot in front of the other as you normally would in a fighting position. Simply stand normally with your feet side by side. Bend your knees slightly.

Now, put your hands up in a fighting position with your fists slightly closed and forearms near your torso (as if you are about to touch gloves or fists with your opponent).

Next, focus on relaxing your body. Take a few slow, deep breaths. Using only your hips--quickly rotate your torso counter clockwise (to the left) as if you are going to throw a punch with your right hand. Do not punch or extend your arm when rotating. Keep your hands near your torso. The focus is solely on generating power from the hips.

The sudden "torque" (twist) of your hips will cause your entire torso to rotate quickly and forcefully. Repeat the hip torque and rotation to the right (clockwise). Although your hips should only move an inch or two--you should feel a tremendous force behind the torque. Complete 5-10 hip rotations in each direction (left and right).

Hip and Shoulder Torquing Drill

For this drill, you will assume the same position (from the previous hip torquing drill). The difference with this drill is that you will actually throw a punch with the hip and torso rotation.

As you complete the sudden hip torque (twist)--use the momentum from your rotating hips and torso to "launch" a punch from your shoulder. You will notice that your punch snaps out as if it is being shot from a cannon. Complete 5-10 torquing punches with each hand.

Be sure to concentrate on feeling the rotation and kinetic linking—in the hips, torso, shoulder, and launch of the punch. Visualize yourself delivering knockout force by putting your entire upper body into the punches.

Full Body Torquing Drill

Once you have the coordination to execute the hip rotation and shoulder launch from a normal standing position, you should proceed to the next step-- torquing from a fighting position. You will add more weight and power to your strikes by adding your legs to the kinetic chain (torquing).

From your fighting position--you can choose to lead with your right side or left side for this drill.

Start by practicing a cross punch. The punch begins with the push off of your back leg to propel yourself forward toward the target. As you push off with your leg—your hips twist violently—and your torso rotation culminates in the shoulder launch and shooting of your right (or left) cross.

Keep your focus on effective synchronization of the rear leg push off, hip twist, torso rotation, shoulder turn, and finally--the whipping power punch. Complete 5-10 repetitions with each side.

Practice the full body torquing drill with your hook punches using the lead hand and rear hand. When using your lead hand for hook punches--you will push off with your front leg as your hips, torso, shoulder, and hook punch rotate inward toward the target. For rear hand hook punches, the torquing starts with pushing off on the rear leg.

Try the torquing drill with a rear leg roundhouse kick from the fighting position. Lastly, practice full body torquing with various power strikes, throws, and takedowns.

When practicing torquing drills, I encourage you to start slower and increase your speed as you get warmed up and more coordinated with the kinetic linking for specific power weapons. Your goal is to practice torquing until the body mechanics and synchronization for each power weapon become automatic.

Barbell Bar Torque

You can use a standard barbell bar to help develop stronger torque and kinetic linking for improved striking and throwing power.

For this exercise, you will need a standard barbell bar and a few towels. Bundle the towels and place them on the floor. Push the towels into a corner. Place the barbell bar on the floor. Push one end of the bar directly into the bundled towels in the corner. Stand facing the end of the barbell bar that is not in the bundled towels. Now, grab the end of the bar with two hands and raise it until it is at chest height. The bar should now be at about a 45-degree angle, and you should be standing straight. Bend your knees slightly and step back until your arms are nearly straight while still holding the barbell with both hands.

Using your arms, shoulders, torso, and hips-- begin to slowly rotate the bar counterclockwise and to your left until it is about one foot from the floor. Be sure to twist your torso, knees, and both feet to the left. Both knees will bend, and the heel of your right foot will naturally lift so that you are on your toes. This is similar to the mechanics of throwing a right cross when all of your body weight shifts to the left. Repeat this exercise going clockwise and to your right. Make sure the bar goes down your right side until it is about one foot from the floor.

Practice ten continuous side-to-side repetitions of the barbell bar twist. This is one set. Take a 30-second break and repeat. You should do a total of 3 sets. To avoid injury and generate maximum power, be sure to keep your back straight throughout the exercise.

As you get more comfortable with this exercise, you can twist the bar faster. This will give the torquing muscles of your hips, core, and shoulders a very effective workout. Simultaneously, this will improve your body mechanics for enhanced power.

As you gain strength and power, add a barbell plate (start with 5 10 pounds) to one end of the bar (closest to you). The added weight will provide more resistance and further strengthen your torquing muscles. Use your clasped hands to keep the barbell plate in place as your raise the bar to start the exercise.

Resistance Bands

Resistance band technology is now widely used by world-class athletes to improve speed, strength, and explosive power.

Resistance bands are rubber or latex, tubes or strips of various lengths and thicknesses with handles on the ends. They come in a variety of styles that provide resistance levels from 3 pounds up to 15 pounds.

If you are not familiar with resistance bands, I suggest you visit a local sporting goods store and try out this valuable tool. Also, check out online videos to get additional ideas on how to use resistance bands for improved strength and power.

Resistance bands provide constant tension as punches and kicks are thrown. This continual resistance allows you to build strength and power throughout the entire movement. In addition, resistance bands will enhance your ability to penetrate or strike *through* the target for greater impact.

Be sure to warm up before you begin resistance band training. Start by using the resistance band for 3 rounds (1 minute each) with your arms—followed by 3 rounds (1 minute each) with your legs.

Experiment with resistance bands by using various power strikes and combinations. Also, engage a training partner to help you develop creative power drills.

Always protect your elbows and knees. Don't lock them out during resistance band exercises (to avoid excess strain). Start with lower resistance levels to enhance your form and encourage proper muscle development before graduating to higher resistance levels.

Shadow Fighting

Shadow fighting (or shadow boxing) is a time-tested training tool for the serious fighter. Shadow fighting provides the following benefits for the combat power student.

* Improves form, coordination, and body mechanics

* Improves kinetic linking and torquing

* Improves relaxation and speed

* Improves balance, footwork, and power base

* Improves focus and killer instinct

* Improves breathing and stamina

Shadow fight for 3-5 minutes (one round), with one minute rest between rounds. Typically, I do three rounds of shadow fighting before equipment training. Shadow fighting prepares you to engage training equipment (and training partners) with maximum focus and force, which will lead to better results and faster progress.

Practice shadow fighting at half speed and progress to full speed as your form, coordination, balance, and stamina improve. Be sure to practice using all of your power weapons--including strikes, throws, takedowns, and submissions.

Shadow fighting is great for sharpening Combat PowerSync and killer instinct. Practice using your imagination by picturing your opponent. Visualize yourself executing a combination of power techniques to knockout or submit your opponent from a variety of ranges.

Do not be too concerned if you initially feel awkward throwing various combinations during shadow fighting. Keep training diligently, and you will see consistent improvement in your coordination and ability to execute power combinations fluidly.

Power Training Tip

To challenge and develop your dynamic balance and power base—try "blind shadow fighting" (shadow fighting with your eyes closed). You will notice that your ability to maintain balance (and a power base) will improve rapidly after practicing blind shadow fighting for a few weeks.

Paper Target

Remember the simple power equation of W (weight) x S (speed) = P (power)? Undoubtedly, you know that applying maximum W (weight) has a lot to do with how effective you are at using body mechanics to leverage all of your available weight for power strikes and throws.

The paper target is a very simple, but highly effective training tool for many combat power students. With this inexpensive tool, you can improve your torquing power and ability to generate superior force.

Start by tying or taping a string to a piece of 8(inch) x 11(inch) standard copy paper. Tie or tape the other end of the string to the ceiling so that the paper is hanging at face height. Using the paper as your target, stand about eight to ten inches away with both of your feet parallel to it. Keeping both loosely clenched fists in front of your chest, elbows hanging freely at your sides, stand with both knees bent. Twist your body clockwise as far as it will go. Now, your body should be facing to your right, 90 degrees from the paper target, with your weight shifting to the left foot. But, your eyes must stay fixed on the paper target.

Now, pivot sharply on the balls of your feet, with your hips initiating a sudden, rotating motion to your left. Your weight quickly shifts to your other foot as your shoulders automatically rotate *after* your hips- -with perfect synchronization. Simultaneously, as your body is rotating, raise your right elbow to your shoulder height just in time to apply an elbow strike to the paper target. The momentum should turn your body 180 degrees, so it faces the opposite or left side. Keep in mind that it is very important that your hips rotate slightly ahead of your shoulder to obtain maximum power.

Repeat the same motion from the left side, striking with your left elbow. Once you have learned to control your torque and begin to feel at ease in this elbow exercise, you can progress to punching.

Step back about 20 to 24 inches from the paper target. Keeping your same body position, twist 90 degrees to the right (clockwise) before rotating 180 degrees back to the left while striking the paper target with a right cross punch.

Be sure to focus on the exaggerated torquing and rotation of your hips. Gradually, to keep your body in balance--especially after the completion of the punch--you can practice striking the paper target from your normal fighting position by placing one foot forward. As your hips initiate the movement, you pivot on the balls of both feet, and your body is driven forward by the impetus from the rear foot. Your rear heel rises as your weight quickly shifts to the front foot with the delivery of the punch, which shoots from the shoulder.

For practicing power kicks, you should apply the same basic rotation principles. In practicing kicking mechanics, you should start by lowering the paper target to your waist height. Focus on really emphasizing hip rotation to generate maximum power when kicking the paper target.

It is important to practice the paper target drills with patience until you have mastered the mechanics of power. Don't waste valuable training time, or develop bad habits on heavier contact training tools (such as the heavy bag), until you have mastered the body mechanics of basic kinetic linking and power generation.

Heavy Bag

The heavy punching bag is the best piece of equipment available for developing striking power and explosiveness. It is a must-have solo training tool for every combat power student.

Heavy bags can range in weight from 40 pounds up to 200 pounds. They are available in a variety of fabrics, shapes, and lengths. If you are planning to purchase a heavy bag, check online for options and pricing.

Unlike punching the air (or paper target)--hitting the heavy bag involves more muscular exertion, which causes fatigue to set in quicker. Naturally, a more fatigued muscle is slower and less powerful. Despite this, you will discover that intense heavy bag work will increase your stamina and ability to maintain power in your strikes for a longer period of time.

Your heavy bag training should consist of 3-5 minute rounds with one minute rest between each round. Start with two or three round of striking. As your stamina improves, you can increase the number of rounds. In order to protect yourself from injury, I recommend wearing protective gloves when training with a heavy bag.

Start your heavy bag training by focusing on individual power strikes. For example—you can start by hitting the bag repeatedly with a right cross. From there, you can focus on developing power in your hook punch--roundhouse kick—elbow strike--knee strike--and headbutt. Start at 50% power on the heavy bag and continue to increase the force until you are hitting with 100% speed and power (without sacrificing form or body mechanics).

Once you have developed sufficient power with all of your individual power strikes--you should proceed to simple and complex combinations in order to develop flow power and improve your Combat PowerSync. You can practice an infinite number of combinations using all of your power striking weapons. Also, you can improve footwork and power base maintenance by delivering power strikes to the heavy bag from a variety of angles and ranges.

To relay peak power--you must think with power and move with power. When working with the heavy bag, you should mentally focus on delivering your strikes with maximum force and determination. Hitting the heavy bag with only light jabs or "slapping" strikes is not productive for the combat power student.

To get the most out of your heavy bag training, you should treat the bag like a real opponent. Circle it—push it—evade it---control the distance--talk to it—and (most of all) don't forget to *crush it with relentless power strikes*!

When training with a heavy bag, it is easy to get carried away and start throwing sloppy haymakers and uncontrolled kicks. It is very important that you develop and maintain good habits of power that align with the power principles. This includes striking with relaxed muscles, a focused mind, effective breathing, good balance, and well-coordinated kinetic linking.

The heavy bag will naturally teach you the power principle of penetration and how to strike through the target. Train yourself to consistently strike *through* the bag a few inches in order to get comfortable with the feeling of impact and displacement.

Do not telegraph punches and kicks by tensing or pulling back first. Telegraphing strikes will diminish your ability to connect with the target in a real fight because your opponent is likely to see the strike coming. Instead, focus on developing a calm, but determined "poker face" that allows you to strike efficiently, quickly, *and* powerfully.

Punching Dummy

Like the heavy bag, the punching dummy is a valuable solo power tool. Training with the punching dummy will complement your heavy bag training. You will focus on developing power while beginning to fill the gap between generating power and connecting with power. Whereas the heavy bag is most effective for developing pure power--the punching dummy starts to develop your accuracy and precision.

I, like many combat fighters, use the punching dummy because it provides a more accurate simulation of striking a real person when compared to other freestanding bags. When striking the punching dummy, you will notice that it feels similar to striking an opponent.

The punching dummy provides realistic target practice, allowing you to focus your power strikes on connecting accurately with the head, chin, throat, and solar plexus. When receiving power combinations, the punching dummy tends to react more like an opponent. An example is the uppercut punch. Because the punching dummy has a chin--it makes practicing this power punch more natural and authentic.

The punching dummy can be filled with sand or water and will typically weight between 200 pounds and 300 pounds when the base is completely filled. It is a versatile tool because the height can be adjusted from 60 inches to 78 inches. Combat students with a limited training area will typically like the punching dummy because it does not require as much space (when compared to a heavy bag)—and does not require attachment to the ceiling.

The most popular version of the punching dummy is Century Bob®, which is manufactured by Century Martial Arts. Century Bob's surface is made out of high-strength plastisol, and it is stuffed with high-density urethane foam. This makes Bob's surface a more accurate representation of the density for an actual person.

Century Bob is available from a wide variety of specialty and general retailers. You can search online for the best deals on punching dummies.

I recommend wearing gloves when training with the punching dummy. Start with one round and progress to three rounds. Each round should be 3-5 minutes with one minute rest between each round. Practice using all of your power weapons. Be sure to concentrate on striking with explosiveness and accuracy.

Pads and Shields

As you develop the ability to generate and connect with power on solo training tools—you will need to progress to more challenging and active tools that require a training partner. I recommend using striking pads and shields in your power training sessions with a partner.

Initially, most fighters use striking pads and shields for developing single strike power. For example, the Thai pads (or Thai elbow pads) are a terrific tool for developing the power mechanics of your roundhouse kick. Because you can focus on mastering torque--and you have the benefit of your training partner providing immediate feedback based on the impact--your power will improve more rapidly when you incorporate striking pads and shields into your training.

Because striking pads and shields can be manipulated by a training partner--you will learn to strike with power while adjusting to an opponent's movement and footwork. Regular training with striking pads and shields will improve your applied power and Combat PowerSync.

Striking pads and shields come in a variety of styles and sizes. Typically, they are curved or contoured to help catch the strikes and feature straps to secure the holder's arms and stabilize the striking surface.

You and your training partner should experiment with a variety of striking pads and shields, from smaller pads that attach to one forearm--to larger body shields that require both forearms or attach to the body. Training with the pads and shields should consist of focused 3-5 minute rounds with one minute rest between each round.

When training with a striking pad or shield, the goal is to develop the ability to relay knockout power while the holder (training partner) is moving slightly.

Do not be too concerned with pinpoint accuracy when using these tools. The goal is to start developing "power on the move" without too much emphasis on advanced accuracy and precision.

Besides developing your power—training with striking pads and shields will improve your reaction speed, distancing and timing. After gaining skill in delivering single power shots—you should ask your training partner to challenge you with more movement and angles.

Power Training Tip

You will get the most out of your training equipment when you are crystal clear on the specific training objective. It helps to take a few minutes to think about this (and discuss it, if you are working with a partner). I refer to this as *tool and attribute linking*. By clarifying the specific objective and benefit of a training tool *before* each training session—you will see faster and more dramatic improvement in your attributes.

Double End Bag

There is so much to be gained from this tricky punching bag! The double end bag is a solo training tool that will develop your ability to connect with power. Regular training with a double end bag will improve your timing, rhythm, accuracy, and speed.

Many advanced combat students believe that the double end bag is one of the solo tools that come close to mimicking the timing and accuracy required for effective striking in a real fight or bout.

Have your ever heard an elite athlete mention that their "rhythm is off" after a long absence from the sport (due to injury or offseason break)? Timing, accuracy, and rhythm are advanced attributes that will enhance your effectiveness in any sport. In combat sports and real fighting--having superior timing, rhythm, and accuracy means that you have the skill to initiate and connect with maximum power (when velocity is at its max and your opponent is most vulnerable).

I'll be the first to admit that the double end bag is not easy to hit. For the beginner, it can be downright frustrating. But, if you will hang in there and keep training with this tool—it will pay great dividends in the form of applied power improvements. With practice--you will learn how to consistently hit the formerly elusive bag with a potent mix of punches, kicks, elbows, and headbutts.

If you can strike the double end bag as it moves toward you--you'll connect with a solid hit even if you strike with less than full force. In contrast--if you strike the double end bag as it moves away from you—there will be little or no impact.

Not only do you have to time the strike for optimal impact--you have to punch or kick accurately (at the center of the bag). If you aim and hit the double end bag in the wrong place—your strike will deflect off the side of the bag, or you will miss it completely.

The double end bag does not care how much power you have generated. If you do not time and aim your strikes with precision--they will not be effective. Now, think about this--If you can't hit a bag that is right in front of you, imagine how much trouble you'll have against an opponent who is moving *and* striking back!

Developing your knockout capability through enhanced timing and accuracy requires the development of fast reflexes and a sharp mind. The double end bag will sharpen your reflexes and fighting mind.

I recommend regular training with a double end bag for a few rounds after you have completed your work on the heavy bag or punching dummy.

Power Training Tip

The double end bag can be frustrating for a beginner (and for some advanced combat students who have not trained with it previously). Be patient and invest the time to get proficient at striking the double end bag. Start slow and speed up your strikes as your rhythm and coordination improve. After a few weeks of focused training on the double end bag--you will notice the difference in your ability to connect with power when sparring or fighting.

Reflex Bag

Similar to the double end bag--the reflex bag is a tool for developing power connection skills. The difference with the reflex bag is that it provides more movement than a double end bag, which can offer a greater challenge to your timing and accuracy.

Some fighters prefer the reflex bag because it is more mobile (freestanding) and potentially convenient (if you don't have a place for a double end bag, which requires attachment to the floor and ceiling).

The freestanding reflex bag has a base filled with sand or water to keep it stable. It is a round, padded bag that sits atop a spring-mounted neck designed to provide quick rebound.

Depending on how hard you strike the bag-- the spring allows for extreme bending motion that may even cause the bag to hit the floor. In addition, the bag can mimic an opponent's punch by coming back at you in a swift motion. In this way, a reflex bag will develop your reflexes—along with your timing and precision.

Practice for 3-5 minutes per round when training with the reflex bag. Some fighters alternate using the reflex bag and double end bag in their training sessions. However, if you are focused on developing your timing or accuracy—you can choose to work both tools in the same training session.

Focus Mitts

Focus mitts have become a very popular training tool for developing applied power, accuracy, and combination fluidity. If you've ever watched a professional boxer training for a bout, you've most likely seen him "working the mitts."

A focus mitt is a padded target attached to a glove. All professional boxers and MMA fighters utilize this training tool. Focus mitt training with a willing and capable partner will significantly improve your applied power and general striking skills.

Beginning students make the mistake of rigidly practicing with the mitts. Inexperienced partners will hold them as if they are a heavy bag or shield. The focus mitts are best used for "active" power training. For the striker, the key is to adapt to the mitts (as they are presented by the holder).

You will need a capable partner to get the most out of focus mitt training. The better your partner is at manipulating focus mitts, the better you will get at hitting them. The idea is to force your mind to instantly strike the pad from any angle that your partner holds it. This develops flow power and elevates Combat PowerSync.

The person holding the focus mitts will typically call out combinations and "feed" the puncher good counter-force while maneuvering and working specific power strikes. Focus mitts are often used as an augment to sparring, with more explicit focus on the puncher than the feeder, especially to develop power striking combinations and defensive maneuvers such as "slipping," "bobbing," and "weaving."

To improve your striking power and timing, you must rely on your training partner (wearing the focus mitts) knowing where to set his hands, as well as knowing how to time the movement of the focus mitts. Your partner should watch you closely and comment on how you can improve your technique between combinations.

Initially, focus mitt training will prove to be the source of much frustration. But, I promise you that, within weeks, you will notice a significant improvement in your coordination, speed, and explosiveness.

Do not cheat yourself! You must be patient and start off slowly and in good form. You can speed up as your adaptation speed and applied power improves. Ask your partner to take note of any bad habits you have--such as telegraphing your punches, losing your power base, or dropping your hands. You want to correct as many bad habits in training as you can because you might not have that opportunity in competition or a real fight.

Here are four tips for the holder or "feeder" of the focus mitts.

1. *Keep them tight.* You want the striker to practice throwing punches, kicks, knees, and elbows to the body and head of an imaginary opponent, so keep the mitts close to your own head and body. Begin by holding the mitts up at face height and about six inches apart from one another. Your elbows

should remain against your body as you're moving the mitts and catching most strikes.

2. *Provide resistance.* You should provide resistance for your partner as you catch strikes. Don't allow your partner to knock your hands back with each strike. As each strike lands, push forward slightly. Don't whack too hard, though! Smacking your partner's hands too hard could potentially injure his hands and wrists.

3. *Give correct mitt position.* Straight punches, like jabs and crosses, should land while the mitts are facing forward. Hooks and uppercuts, though, require that you turn the mitts appropriately. For hooks "to the head," turn the palm of the mitt inward in front of your face. For hooks "to the body," place your hand just above your hip with the palm facing outward. For uppercuts, turn your palm downward. Uppercuts often require you to lift your elbows slightly off your body.

4. *Be in command.* You are in control as the holder. You and your partner can assign numbers to punches and/or combinations so that you can call out a number, and the striker can land the appropriate strikes. By controlling the mitts, you can give yourself time to brace for each incoming strike.

5. *Move around.* In a fight—rarely do the combatants stand flat-footed. They stick, move, avoid punches, and stick again. As the holder of the mitts, you can mimic an opponent by moving around between combinations. Also, don't be afraid to throw a few simulated punches of your own. This allows the mitt striker to hone both his offensive and defensive techniques.

I highly recommend finding a competent boxing instructor or purchasing a quality training video that can instruct you on the basics of focus mitt training, holding, and striking. As you (and your training partner) become more comfortable with the mitts—you can begin to train more intensely and creatively. Continue to challenge and push yourself during focus mitt training sessions, and you will develop power combinations that are more instinctive and fluid.

Power Training Tip

Consider having the holder or feeder of the focus mitts wear a body protector to allow for more powerful attacks by the striker. A body protector guards the holder's torso area from potentially harmful power shots.

Medicine Ball

Grappling and wrestling require explosive power for successful throws and takedowns. Also, grappling and ground fighting success demands superior conditioning.

Prolonged periods of grappling in a fight takes tremendous stamina and muscular endurance that can only be developed using specific training tools and programs. Olympic level wrestlers are widely known and respected for their potent combination of strength, power, endurance, and speed.

Fast twitch muscles are critical for explosive power movements (such as power lifting). If you want to become a power grappler who is capable of winning fights with quick submissions, you must develop the fast twitch muscle fibers in your core and posterior chain. The posterior chain is the chain of muscles along the backside, which includes the calves, hamstrings, gluteus maximus, lower back, middle back, trapezius, and rear deltoid muscles. A strong posterior chain is essential for powerful throws and takedowns.

Power grapplers--like power strikers--understand the importance of good form and body mechanics in maximizing leverage and force. They need explosive power to be able to quickly lift and throw an opponent.

The medicine ball is one of the most versatile and beneficial pieces of workout equipment for developing close quarter combat explosiveness. It used to be that the medicine ball was only thought of as a simulated striking tool for developing a fighter's ability to withstand blows to the body.

Today, medicine balls are used by non-combat athletes and can be found in many fitness classes due to their effectiveness in developing core strength and stamina. They come in various sizes (from 6 pounds to 60 pounds), and some even come with handles that can be used for a better grip and a greater variety of exercises.

What I like best about medicine balls for the combat power student is that they are designed to be thrown. Unlike dumbbells, or heavy bags, that will most likely get damaged if you drop them--medicine balls are resilient and allow you to throw them around while training your body to be more powerful and explosive.

Another great thing about medicine balls is that they can be used for core strength and stability training (you know, those muscles that are key to kinetic linking and generating knockout power).

You should start your medicine ball training with a weight that is comfortable and not likely to cause any strain or injury. As you get stronger, you can progress to train with heavier balls. The following medicine ball drills will improve your takedown and submission power.

Floor Slams

This is a very good exercise for developing an explosive core for improved power. I recommend doing this exercise outdoors or in a ground floor gym.

To start, snatch the ball up over your head. Once the ball is over your head, swing downward and slam the ball into the floor as hard as you can--all the while keeping control of the ball.

You can start by slamming the ball down directly in front of you. From there, you can slam the ball down at different angles to work different areas of your core and simulate a variety of takedowns. Try slamming the ball diagonally down, and then slam it to your side. Remember to control the ball on the way down as you would an opponent.

Repeat this drill as many times as you can for about 30 seconds. Rest and repeat the exercise for a total of 3 – 5 sets. As your stamina improves, you can reduce the rest period.

Rotational Throws

This drill will develop your rotational power for throwing and striking. You will need an open and spacious area to perform this drill. I like to practice this drill outdoors.

Start with the ball low near your left foot and proceed to toss it over the back of your right shoulder. Perform the opposite movement pattern. Perform 2 sets of 6 to 10 reps. This will not only develop power in your core, glutes, back, and legs—but also, it will work your heart and lungs.

Straight Throws

This medicine ball drill will help you develop more power in your punches, throws, and takedowns.

Holding the medicine ball with both hands-- stagger your stance, so the right foot is back slightly. Rotate to your right and draw the medicine ball back while loading up power in the core, shoulders, and arms. Now explode by swiveling your hips and torso to fire the ball forward as fast as you can.

Perform 2 sets of 6 to 8 reps with each arm. Be careful to practice this in an open area where there is no risk of injury to people or walls.

As a dedicated combat power student, I urge you to explore more resources on how to use the medicine ball for improving your power in grappling, ground fighting, and striking.

Grappling Dummy

The grappling dummy is a solo training tool that will improve your ability to finish off an opponent with power throws, takedowns, and submissions. As a power training tool—the grappling dummy is beneficial to grappling and ground fighting in the same way that a punching dummy is beneficial to striking.

A grappling dummy is especially helpful when you don't have a training partner available, and you want to practice grappling and ground positioning. There are literally hundreds of techniques you can do with a grappling dummy--including throws, takedowns, ground and pound, chokes, and locks.

You can work on your top control game by doing various position changes while on top of the dummy. And, you can even pull guard with the dummy as a warm up for practicing with a training partner.

As a conditioning bonus---intense workouts with the grappling dummy will tax your stamina and develop your ability to maintain power.

One of the best features of the grappling dummy is that you can throw it, kick it, and punch it--and it just keeps getting up for more! The grappling dummy doesn't mind being subjected to your powerful ground and pound! All combat students, including Brazilian Jiu Jitsu specialists--Judokas--MMA fighters—and reality self-defense practitioners—should try using the grappling dummy to develop superior power.

For me personally, I was a little bit skeptical when it came to the use of a grappling dummy. Despite my initial reservations, I sought out a mixed martial arts gym that was stocked with various grappling dummies. I started doing repetition after repetition of my favorite power throws and takedowns. Subsequently, I discovered that the power I was generating when throwing a resisting opponent increased significantly. Needless to say--grappling dummy drills are now a permanent part of my training program.

There are different styles of grappling dummies, and they can vary in weight from 20 pounds up to 140 pounds. Available options include the following:

*Basic heavy bags with contoured centers to represent the torso (doubles as a grappling dummy and a punching bag). Some designs include handles on the top and side for lifting and throwing.

*Standing dummies with head, legs, and arms (for general-purpose grappling)

*Seated dummies with head, legs, and arms (for ground fighting, positioning, and submissions)

If you don't have access to a grappling dummy at a local gym, you can purchase one from an online retailer--or at your local sporting equipment store.

I recommend breaking down your grappling dummy training into the following categories:

1. Clinches (infighting, knees, elbows, and headbutts)

2. Throws (slams, arm throws, leg throws, and hip throws; some judokas dress the grappling dummy in a gi to simulate throwing an opponent in competition)

3. Takedowns (one leg, two-legged, arm, and neck takedowns; open mat and from the cage wall)

4. Position Training (mounting and guarding)

5. Ground & Pound (punches, elbows, knees, and headbutts)

6. Submissions (chokes, arm bars, leg bars, and joint locks)

7. Free Flow (combinations of clinches, throws, takedowns, positioning, ground striking, and submissions).

Start out by training with the grappling dummy on power techniques and form for each category listed above. From there, you should progress to work with the grappling dummy for 3 rounds of 3-5 minutes with one minute rest between rounds.

Contact Sparring

Sparring is a form of training that is common to all combat styles. It is "free flow" fighting, with varying rules designed to prevent serious injury. Contact sparring is critical to your total power development! It represents the best imitation of real fighting (for sport or self-defense).

Bruce Lee said that martial artists who train without contact sparring are "dry land swimming." At some point--if you want to learn how to swim--you will eventually have to jump into the water. Similarly, I don't believe you can actually learn how to fight with power--unless you experience the emotion and blunt force of a fight first hand (using protective gear and semi-controlled circumstances).

The more closely sparring represents the actual event (fight)--the more effective it will be in preparing you to apply knockout power in the midst of a more serious combat situation. When done realistically, contact sparring will hone and optimize your Combat PowerSync.

Although contact sparring is not actual combat, it will familiarize you with the ranges, adrenaline rush, discomfort, and unpredictable flow of combat. But, keep in mind that you cannot use some of the most effective self-defense techniques (eye gouging, biting, groin strikes, throat strikes, and joint breaks) when sparring. You can develop power in these more vicious self-defense techniques by practicing on solo training equipment.

Combat Readiness

You have learned that relaxation is an essential prerequisite for power (and success) in fighting. Realistic full-contact sparring will train you to relax at will--even in the heat of a competitive physical battle.

Relaxation skill in combat depends on the cultivation of mental focus and emotional poise in the midst of chaos. The kind of relaxation you are concerned with is that of the body--not the mind. In sparring or combat--your mind should be intensely focused on decimating your opponent--while your body should be relaxed, supple, and ready to explode in an instant.

Sparring Gear

The clear purpose of this book is to help you develop the skills to generate and connect with devastating knockout power. With power comes responsibility. When training with a partner, you should take precautions to make sure no serious injuries result from contact sparring.

Protecting participants during full contact sparring requires quality sparring gear. The following protective equipment will allow you and your training partners to spar safely *and* with power. Most gear comes in a variety of styles, sizes, and colors.

*Headgear (protects head and face; open face or full face for more coverage)

*Sparring Gloves (protect hands, fists, and wrists; exposed or covered fingers)

*Mouth Guard (protects jaw and teeth; single piece or double piece)

*Support Cup (protects groin area; cup only or cup within compression shorts)

*Chest Guard (protects chest, stomach, ribs, and groin)

*Boots / Shoes (protects foot, toes, and provides traction)

*Shin Guards (protects shin and instep)

Sparring Drills

In order to fully exploit the benefits of sparring--I recommend experimenting with a variety of sparring drills, including the following five types:

1. *Full Speed.* All out one-on-one sparring with full contact (and gear).

2. *Half Speed.* Slower sparring intended to develop the form, techniques, and body mechanics that will contribute to increased power in full speed sparring.

3. *Blind.* Sparring with blindfolds (during clinching and grappling activity) is very effective for developing your balance, relaxation, kinetic linking, power base, and flow power (ability to exploit your opponent's movement and energy).

4. *Footwork.* Upright sparring without striking or contact. The goal is to develop dynamic balance and power-base skills that will keep you in a position to attack with knockout power. If you want to maintain punching distance and your partner takes one step forward--you take one step back. If he steps or circles to the left--you step or circle to the right. In boxing, this footwork synchronization with the opponent is called "cutting off the ring."

5. *Situational.* Unlike full speed sparring--situational sparring calls for non-traditional full-contact fighting scenarios that are designed to challenge and cultivate your adaptability skills. Most fighters are proficient when defending against a particular style of fighter, in a particular type of setting. However, a superior power fighter is one who can successfully adapt to any style of fighting--in any

situation--and still deliver a knockout. That is the essence of Combat PowerSync.

Examples of situational sparring include: sparring against multiple attackers; sparring against new training partners who come from different styles; sparring against a street fighter; sparring with one hand tied behind your back (to simulate a broken arm); sparring from a seated position (to simulate being attacked while in a chair); sparring against an opponent with a weapon.

During situational sparring--your goal is to create unfamiliar situations and to respond as quickly, accurately, and powerfully as possible. Work with your training partners to come up with a variety of scenarios that could arise in the ring or street. Put your imagination to work--the potential situations are endless. Have fun with it, and your sparring will be more enjoyable, motivating and productive.

You should spar in a variety of combat ranges in order to develop knockout and submission power for any situation. This will give you a definite advantage over an opponent who is skilled in only one or two ranges.

Start introducing range-specific contact sparring into your training as a way to master your favorite submission and knockout weapons for each range. Study and use the Combat Range Matrix to create clarity and focus when training for the 20 ranges of contact.

With range-specific power training--you will develop an instinctive "range sensitivity" that will automatically trigger you to use the most appropriate knockout and submission weapons.

Power Training Tip

Getting clocked (hit hard) is a natural fear for most people. However, this fear must be controlled if you want to become a superior power fighter. Be sure to spar with capable partners who can hit and submit with power so that you learn to "take it—or evade it" as well as you can "dish it out."

Don't be the person who only wants to spar with inferior, low-power opponents. The more you challenge yourself (within safe limits)--the faster you will see growth in your power, skills, and confidence.

Chapter 7

Supplemental Power Training

If you are serious about doubling or tripling your combat power (and I know you are)--you will need to get your body and mind into top condition. Supplemental training knowledge can help you reach your full potential as a power fighter.

This chapter provides highlights on the latest science in strength, endurance, nutrition, and mental training. In addition, you will learn useful tips on how to use stretching to get more flexible and improve your overall fighting capabilities.

Strength Training

As a knockout and submission fighter--you need to be strong. You don't need to post world-class numbers from a powerlifting standpoint, but you will be more powerful if you possess excellent strength (based on your size, gender, and age).

High levels of strength will improve the amount of force you can produce throughout your entire body. Some fighters focus on conditioning and avoid pure strength training. This is a big mistake. Strength provides a foundation for potential power.

With increased strength—you have more capacity for delivering knockouts and submissions.

Training with heavy free weights is the most effective method for increasing muscular strength. It was once thought that lifting weights would make you slow and compromise your skill, timing, and coordination. That notion--as science and many great athletes have repeatedly shown--has been completely invalidated.

All of today's top fighters supplement their skill and attribute training with weight lifting--and, as a result--today's fighters are stronger, faster, and more powerful than ever before. For the combat power student--weight training will provide the following specific benefits:

*Increased penetration power

*Increased speed and explosiveness

*Increased grappling strength

*Increased muscular endurance

To get started with weight training--you can invest in quality equipment, or you can join a health club that has quality equipment. I like to use my local health club because they maintain state-of-the-art weight lifting equipment, which can be expensive to purchase.

Below are three critical weight training tips for fighters who want to increase applied strength for striking and grappling.

1. Focus on Building Strength

2. Lift Heavy

3. Stick to Basics

Now, let's cover each tip in more detail so that you can apply it in your training.

1. *Focus on Building Strength.* Without question, one of the biggest problems for fighters and combat athletes who are trying to get stronger is trying to develop strength and endurance at the same time. Recent research has shown that this approach leads to less than optimal results in both strength and conditioning. A better approach (particularly for beginners) is to isolate the training of these critical attributes into separate workouts.

To build strength—you need to develop a focused and specific strength training program. Save the conditioning and cardiovascular endurance work for separate training sessions where you can really focus on it.

2. *Lift Heavy.* In order to get stronger, you must lift heavy weights. This means you will need to use quality equipment. There are many inferior gadgets on the market that claim to be effective for strength training. The truth is--none of these "infomercial gadgets" will improve your strength faster or more effectively than free weights. What Olympic-level champion or professional athlete have you heard of, who attributes his strength and explosiveness to the latest infomercial exercise gadget?

Free weights force you to balance the weight of the barbell or dumbbells. The extra balancing effort exerted by your muscles forces them to adapt and respond by growing stronger more quickly. For most combat athletes--10-14 focused sets of free weight training for the entire body--with 5-8 quality reps per set--is generally enough to get the job done and see consistent strength improvements.

3. *Stick to Basics.* With the amount of extra time available for strength work often limited, you have to get the most out of your time. This

means you should stick to the basic compound lifts.

To improve your general and functional strength quickly--you should use the big lifts—such as squats, deadlifts, bench presses, clean and jerk, military presses, barbell curls, and barbell rows. These lifts use many different muscles and help improve your nervous system's ability to activate a lot of muscle at once--which provides the foundation for both maximum strength and explosive power.

High emphasis on exercises that isolate small muscle groups—require high reps and sets—or use lighter weight--should be left to bodybuilders and fitness models. If you want to get super strong and develop superior knockout and submission power--focus most of your strength training sessions on proven, basic exercises using heavy free weights.

Power Training Tip

Recommendation: John Jesse authored one of the finest books on strength training and conditioning I have ever read. It is titled *Wrestling Physical Conditioning Encyclopedia*. The book is currently out of print, but you can check online to find a used copy. If you are a wrestler, grappler, or just want to achieve exceptional strength and physical fitness--you should definitely check out this classic book.

Endurance

Cardiovascular (cardio) exercise is the best way to strengthen your most important muscle--the heart. By increasing your heart strength, you will increase your endurance and stamina--which increases your ability to sustain power for longer periods of time.

Endurance training should be a high priority on every power fighter's training schedule!

Contrary to what some "death touch" advertisements claim, most fights will not end with one killer move. Often, in a real fight--stamina and endurance will be the limiting factor of your effectiveness.

When you are tired--power, speed and everything else goes out the window! In fact—a lack of endurance and stamina will hinder all of your other attributes. When you are fatigued--you are weaker, slower, more careless, and less precise in your thoughts and actions.

Combat endurance capacity will influence the application of skill and execution of technique. A well-conditioned combat athlete can fight consistently and effectively with the least effort.

Endurance can be divided into two categories--*general endurance* (applies to any activity) and *specific endurance* (applies to the specific sport or skill). An example of a general endurance exercise for the combat power student is jogging. An example of a specific endurance exercise for the combat power student is heavy bag training.

Endurance training can be either aerobic (with oxygen), or anaerobic (without oxygen). Although fighting is almost purely anaerobic, you should use cardiovascular exercise in the form of aerobics as the foundation of your endurance training.

To get adequate aerobic exercise, physiologists tell us that we should raise our pulse to the *target zone* for at least 20 to 30 minutes--and that we should do this at least 3 times a week. You can find your target zone by first subtracting your age from 220. This number represents your estimated maximum heart rate.

For example--if you are a 20-year-old male--your maximum heart rate is 200 beats per minute (220 minus 20 = 200). Now, multiply the difference (200) by 0.6 to get your target low--and multiply the difference by 0.8 to get your target high. In this example, the 20-year-old has a target low of 120 beats per minute (.6 x 200)—and a target high of 160 beats per minute (.8 x 200).

You are advised to keep your pulse within the target zone when exercising aerobically. Raising your target heart rate to higher levels (above 85 percent of your maximum heart rate) is considered anaerobic and should only be done after you have attained a basic level of fitness through regular aerobic exercise.

A commonly used barometer for determining if you are exercising aerobically or anaerobically is the "talk test." If you can carry on a normal conversation without much effort during exercise--you are exercising aerobically. If you can barely speak during exercise—you are exercising anaerobically.

High-intensity anaerobic exercise will help you develop stamina for sustained power and improved Combat PowerSync. Gradually, you should begin to insert anaerobic bursts or high-speed intervals into your cardiovascular training program. The anaerobic bursts will improve your aerobic capacity—and they will simulate the bursts of energy necessary to overpower and finish an opponent during a fight.

As you begin implementing anaerobics, you will experience an uncomfortable ache in your muscles. The goal is to make this feeling of discomfort so familiar that it becomes an ally in competition and self-defense.

Well-trained wrestlers and grapplers have high levels of specific anaerobic endurance. I have watched marathon runners end up completely out of gas after grappling for a couple of rounds. Marathoners have high levels of aerobic endurance. They do not necessarily have high levels of the specific anaerobic endurance found in wrestlers and grapplers.

To develop specific anaerobic endurance for combat--you should practice full contact sparring and grappling with someone who has more strength and stamina than you do. Fighting an opponent with superior strength and stamina will really tax your body and mind. You will have to learn how to control your breathing and relax your muscles when not attacking or defending. But, stick with it, and you will quickly notice improvements in your endurance and ability to sustain power for the duration of a fight.

Power Training Tip

You can accelerate the development of your endurance by using a specialized tool called *Power*

Lung®. I use this tool regularly to support endurance development and maintenance. Power Lung is a respiratory strength training machine.

There are muscles that support your breathing. Just like any other muscle in your body, the best way to make them stronger and more efficient is to strength train them using progressive resistance. Power Lung is designed to train and strengthen your inhalation and exhalation breathing muscles.

I suggest you go online and check it out. I have found Power Lung to be particularly effective in helping me break through plateaus in my endurance training.

Flexibility

Most combat athletes practice and train diligently when it comes to the development of technical skill and the attributes of speed and power. However, they often neglect proper stretching and sometimes lack sufficient flexibility to perform techniques with peak efficiency.

The best way to improve flexibility is through consistent and progressive stretching. Proper stretching increases range of motion and flexibility by lengthening soft tissues, such as muscles and ligaments. It promotes fluid movement during athletic performance and minimizes injury.

The more flexible you are--the more relaxed your muscles will be--and the faster you can move without risking injury. A fighter who is flexible has more body control, which is essential for initiation speed and movement speed. And of course, you now know that a faster fighter is a more powerful fighter.

An active warm up of 5-10 minutes at low to moderate aerobic intensity should be done prior to stretching. Be sure to avoid bouncing during a stretch--and do not overstretch your muscles. Stretching should be a calm and enjoyable activity that relaxes your body.

There are two basic types of stretching--static and dynamic. Static stretching requires you to move a muscle to the end of its range of motion and maintain it without pain for 20-60 seconds. During static stretching, you should concentrate on relaxing the target muscles and breathing deeply.

Dynamic stretching involves active tightening of muscles to move joints through their full range of motion. It works by gently propelling your muscles towards their maximum range of motion. In general, you are moving and stretching muscles similar to the way they will move in training or fighting. For example—doing slow, light kicks while gradually increasing the height is a dynamic stretch.

Dynamic stretching can be used as part of your warm-up routine before all-out training. During dynamic stretching--focus on smooth and relaxed movements that do not shock or strain the muscles. Do not use jerky, forced movements to increase the range of motion beyond what is comfortable as it can easily cause injury.

Everyone has different needs when it comes to stretching. Get to know which of your joints are loose and supple, and which are tight and less supple. You can make more effective use of your time by concentrating on the stretching exercises that will increase flexibility of the joints that need it most.

There are many factors that determine your flexibility--age, genetics, gender, training program, fitness level, and muscle tone--just to name a few. The key is to focus your time and energy on those factors that you can influence. Never waste your valuable time on factors that you have no control over.

A regular stretching program will help you maintain flexibility and readiness for competition and self-defense. I recommend a balanced and progressive stretching program to help you prevent injuries and prepare your body for optimal training and competitive performance. There are many helpful books available on proper stretching. Check your favorite online bookstores for options.

Diet and Nutrition

Being a combat athlete--you want to feel your best in order to get the most out of your training. Good basic nutrition is a prerequisite to health, fitness, and high performance.

A leaner athlete is a faster and more explosive athlete. Excessive body fat will hinder your speed. You should strive to achieve reasonably low levels of body fat through consistent training and a healthy diet.

Do not become fanatical with losing every ounce of body fat. Some body fat is necessary for good health and adequate energy levels. You must also consider genetics. Some people are meant to be leaner than others. Just do what you can to achieve your optimum weight and level of body fat. This is the level at which you feel your best and most capable as a fighter.

Your diet should be built on common sense. For starters--avoid foods that are high in saturated fat, trans fat, hydrogenated oils, excessive salt (sodium), and refined sugar. The key is to avoid unhealthy foods and nutrients as much as possible. Lastly, you should avoid foods that are known allergens (check with your doctor or an allergist to find out if you have any specific food allergies).

The foods and nutrients at the foundation of your diet should be generally high in fiber, protein, vitamins, minerals, complex carbohydrates, and healthy fats. Try to eat something from all healthy food groups at every major meal. This will ensure that you are getting all of the proper nutrients to fuel your training.

Strive to increase your consumption of water, vegetables, and fresh fruits. Simultaneously, you should decrease and minimize your consumption of sugar-laden beverages, sugary and fatty desserts, candy, and fast foods.

Learn how to substitute healthy food alternatives for less healthy foods. There are now more delicious, healthier alternatives to traditionally high-calorie foods than ever before. Work on continuous improvement in your diet by educating yourself on how to make healthy eating choices— such as how to shop for and prepare healthy foods, and how to eat healthy when dining out.

Drink plenty of pure water every day. It is the most vital nutrient of basic health. Substitute fresh water in place of sodas and artificial juices. Consider zero calorie vitamin water and sodas as a way to get the taste without the sugar and empty calories. This alone can help you shed unwanted pounds that might slow you down and decrease your explosiveness.

Like many people—I am constantly balancing multiple factors related to diet and nutrition, including—taste preferences, cost, convenience, calories, conflicting news, social pressures, and varying family dietary requirements. My advice is to avoid becoming fanatical about your diet. Instead, keep it simple and focus on stressing healthy variety in your daily meals, while staying conscious and aware of how your diet makes you feel and perform (physically and mentally).

Combat athletes tend to view eating and food as *fuel for the body*. Those with poor diet habits tend to view food and eating as an emotional pleasure or distraction.

It is okay to take frequent, small drinks of water during your workouts. If possible, you should choose filtered water. If your training or exercise sessions are longer than 60 minutes, you should consider a quality sports drink to replace electrolytes, potassium, and carbohydrates.

The best way to evaluate a food is to be acutely aware of how it affects you physically and mentally. Do you feel sluggish? Is your stomach upset? Are you more energetic? Is your concentration improved? On a daily basis, you must decide which foods will fuel your body. The results of your decisions will be evident in how you look, feel, and perform.

Supplements

Many boxers, wrestlers, and MMA competitors use nutritional supplements to help maintain their basic health and support their training regimens.

Despite the best intentions to eat a well-balanced diet every day, the majority of people will fall short. At a minimum, nutritional supplements offer insurance against nutritional deficiency. Optimally, nutritional supplements can improve function and performance.

Ideally, you should take a vitamin deficiency test to see if any vitamins or minerals are lacking in your daily diet. You can then take the vitamins and minerals you need to make up for the deficiency. This test will also prevent you from spending money on supplements you don't need. Search online for a local and licensed nutritionist. If you cannot locate a nutritionist, ask your physician to test you for vitamin deficiencies, or refer you to someone who can.

If your diet is well-balanced--the overwhelming odds are that you will not be deficient in any vitamins or minerals. However, as an active combat athlete, your nutritional needs may vary from the sedentary population.

I will avoid recommending a particular brand of vitamins. I will just say that a good multivitamin that includes all of the necessary daily nutrients is a good start. You can try additional products to see if they enhance your health and fitness, but you should consult your physician.

It is important to have a sufficient supply of all B-vitamins to make sure your muscles and reflexes are functioning at their peak. B-vitamins aid in converting carbohydrates into glucose, and are necessary for the normal functioning of the nervous system.

In addition to B-vitamins, it is critical that you have sufficient protein in your diet to help develop and maintain muscular strength for improved power. Check with your local health store to learn more about various protein supplements. Knowledgeable store personnel can help you compare options and choose the best protein supplement to meet your needs.

Because nutritional supplements can be expensive and sometimes dangerous, you should be wary of heavily advertised supplements that are promoted with outlandish or unproven claims. If you have questions about a supplement, talk to your physician or qualified health care professional.

Mental Training

Mental training is indispensable for the superior fighter. Often, those fighters with the highest level of physical skill seem to possess the most advanced mental capabilities for effective fighting. This is no accident. To become a knockout power fighter, you must develop the ability to maintain focus and unwavering confidence in the midst of brutal combat.

By training your mind and body effectively, you will make sure your opponent is not able to break your will or make you give up in a fight. Conversely, you will learn to use your mind to help break down an opponent's desire and set him up for a decisive knockout or submission.

Meditation is a proven tool for developing mental power for combat. Regular practice of this ancient exercise increases your ability to maintain the optimal mental and emotional state during intense combat situations. Meditation can effectively integrate relaxation, breathing, visual imagery, self-talk, and self-hypnosis.

There are many schools of thought on the science of meditation, but the end result is always the same--*the simultaneous achievement and sustainment of a relaxed body and focused mind.*

Meditation is a simple exercise. First, you should find a comfortable position. This can be lying down, sitting, or standing. Close your eyes. Now, tense your whole body as hard as you can, from the top of your head to the bottom of your feet. Hold this for about 5-10 seconds, and then relax.

Next, take three deep breaths. Be sure to breathe slowly and naturally. Inhale deeply and exhale slowly, while pursing your lips. During the first exhalation, softly say, "Legs relax," and think and feel your legs relaxing. During the second exhalation, softly say, "Arms relax," and think and feel your arms relaxing. During the third exhalation, softly say, "Body relax," and think and feel your entire body relaxing.

If any part of you remains tense, go back and relax it by softly telling that part of your body to relax.

Concentrate on keeping your breathing slow, deep, and rhythmic until you feel totally relaxed from head to toe.

At this point, you should begin to program yourself using self-hypnosis. You can do this by repeating the following suggestion at least ten times: "My total fighting power continues to improve every day."

The statement I prepared for you is for general power development. It can be altered as necessary to suit your needs. If you wanted to focus on improving one specific component of your Combat PowerSync, you could build your statement around that.

For instance--"My torquing power continues to improve every day."

Athletes from all major sports have successfully used self-hypnosis to improve attributes and enhance their skills.

While meditating, you should practice visualizing yourself as you want to be. Concentrate intensely on seeing yourself as having knockout power. The scenes should look so realistic that it is like you are watching yourself in a movie.

Practice brief meditation once or twice a day. After you become more proficient, you will not need to practice as often. In the beginning stages, you can meditate while lying down. Once you become proficient at relaxing your body—you will be able to meditate anywhere, at any time.

Some fighters find that the best time to practice meditation, self-hypnosis, and visual imagery is just before falling asleep and immediately upon arising in the morning. At these times, you are in a natural state of relaxation, and the suggestions will sink in more easily. You can also practice self-hypnosis mediation before or after your training sessions.

The goal is to effectively input the suggestions into your subconscious. Once there, the suggestions will start to materialize through the awesome power of believing.

Be certain that your suggestions are clearly spoken. Also, be sure to put as much "feeling" into the suggestions as possible. You must talk like you really believe every word! This belief will cause the suggestions to take on the power of imperial commands. If you simply mouth the words half-heartedly, I guarantee you will be disappointed with the results. Remember, it's often not what you say, but how you say it that matters.

Meditation, along with visual imagery, directed self-talk, and focused self-hypnosis will do wonders for your physical skills. The change will not take place overnight, but there will be a noticeable change in as little time as ten days.

Initially, you may not notice improvements, but your training partners will. They will feel the change in your power and skill when they spar against you. They will observe that you seem more confident and relaxed, but they will not know why unless you tell them about your mental training exercises.

To learn more, I suggest you check out a few articles and books on mental training and conditioning for combat. Advanced combat students are continuous learners! You can incorporate the knowledge and drills that are most beneficial into your regular training sessions and daily life.

Chapter 8

Avoiding The Knockout and Submission

For the combat power student and superior fighter, understanding how to win by knockout is just one side of a two-sided fighting equation. Equally important is the understanding of how to avoid being knocked out by power shots or taken down and defeated by powerful submissions.

In this chapter, I will cover 18 solutions for avoiding defeat by knockout or submission. Incorporating these helpful tips, exercises, and drills into your training program (to be covered in the next chapter) is highly recommended.

Solutions for knockout and submission prevention can be broken down into the following four categories:

1. Pre-Fight (before the fight starts)

2. Pre-Contact (after the fight starts, before the moments of impact)

3. On Contact (the moments of impact)

4. Post-Contact (immediately after impact)

Pre-Fight Solutions

Improve Your Defense

It's often said that a good offense is the best defense.

I agree that possessing knockout power provides a boost of confidence and can serve to intimidate an informed opponent. However, *your* knockout power has nothing to do with your *opponent's* knockout power!

The basic objective in fighting is to *hit and control without getting hit and controlled.* Having very good defensive skills is one of the best solutions for avoiding a knockout or submission. Develop specific drills with your partner to practice blocking, slipping, holding, and escaping—include power strikes, throws, takedowns, and submissions. To improve your defense--you must allocate time to focus on defensive strategies and skills in your training.

Improve Your Reflexes

Superior reflexes are not just for the genetically gifted. You can--and should--work on improving your reflexes if you want to become a superior fighter.

Great reflexes allow you to see power moves coming (and thus avoid them). With quick reflexes—you make it more difficult for your opponent to catch (surprise) you with a knockout strike. Lastly, superior reflexes will improve your knockout capabilities because you will be able to spot vital target openings sooner.

Check out my book *Speed Training for Combat* to learn more about how to improve your speed and reflexes.

Spar Full Contact

Experience is the best way to learn how to absorb and recover quickly from a power strike or submission technique. Be sure to use protective gear for full-contact sparring—and go all-out so that you can experience defending and countering full power attacks.

Getting comfortable with receiving power and not panicking is an important fighting skill that cannot be fully appreciated and internalized unless you engage in regular full-contact sparring.

Cross Train

Usually, a successful knockout by striking will include an element of surprise. When you are not familiar with the fighting style or preferred combat range of an opponent—your odds of being surprised by a power move will increase. This is the case even if your opponent is not as fast or powerful as you are.

Make it a habit (at least occasionally) to train and spar with fighters from different styles. It's amazing how certain styles emphasize certain power moves, rhythms, angles, and ranges. Learning to adapt to various fighting styles will dramatically decrease your susceptibility to a knockout—especially when your opponent has inferior physical attributes.

Stay in Shape

High levels of endurance and stamina can help you avoid knockouts and submissions. A tired fighter is more likely to be caught off guard and overwhelmed during a combination power attack.

Physical fitness is a cornerstone of all superior fighters and combat champions. Plus, in a self-defense situation--high levels of endurance can save your life by providing you with the extra energy to successfully outrun and escape one or more deadly attackers.

Increase Body Strength

A stronger fighter who can leverage more muscular force is a more powerful fighter. Plus, a stronger fighter is more difficult to knock out or submit. Focus on progressive strength gains and you will decrease your odds of losing the grappling battle with your opponent. By the way—statistics show that more than 90% of real street fights end up on the ground. Be prepared!

Stay Flexible

Increased flexibility will help improve your defensive skills against attempted strikes and submissions. With increased flexibility—you will be more elastic, nimble, and elusive. Be sure to incorporate static and dynamic stretching into your training program.

Learn Grappling

If you are a pure striker--it is very important that you learn grappling skills in order to become a well-rounded power fighter. Unlike other ranges--grappling and ground fighting can be forced upon you by an opponent at any time. Not being familiar with power throws, takedowns, chokes, and joint locks make a pure striker very vulnerable against a multi-range combat power fighter. Learn grappling to improve your Combat PowerSync and stop submissions.

Avoid Street Fights

I do not condone street fighting. However, I fully condone the application of knockout techniques—if necessary to defend yourself or your family members. In other words--don't *start* a street fight--but make sure you are very capable of *ending* a street fight!

The best way to avoid being knocked out in a street fight is to *avoid street fights*! Train yourself to spot potentially volatile situations--and stay away from places that are known to be statistically more dangerous and violent. Ignoring this simple solution will exponentially increase your odds of being knocked out--or worse! Commit to being a confident, smart, responsible, and *safe* combat student.

Pre-Contact Solutions

Control Fear

It is natural to experience fear when fighting. The key is to control this fear. Left uncontrolled--fear can become paralyzing--which can lead to a quick knockout by a power fighter who can sense the opponent's fear.

Use meditation and full-contact sparring to learn how to transform natural fear and adrenaline into controlled killer instinct.

Keep Your Hands Up

A golden rule in boxing is to "protect yourself at all times." This starts with keeping your hands up (to protect your head) and your forearms in (to protect your vital body organs). Showboating or carrying your hands low and out of position will only increase your chances of getting blasted by your opponent.

Keep Your Head Moving

It is a scientific fact that a moving target is harder to hit than a stationary target. In the midst of a fight, you should keep your head moving constantly to create a more challenging target for your opponent.

Practice bobbing, weaving, and effective head movement during sparring sessions--and when training with power equipment. Make head movement a habit during training and it will carry over to your fights.

Keep Your Mouth Closed

With the chin and jaw being prime vital targets for a knockout--boxers learn very early in their training--to keep their mouth closed (and teeth clenched) when fighting. Having your mouth wide open makes it far easier for your opponent to score a knockout if he can connect with a clean punch. Make it a habit to keep your mouth closed during training and fighting.

Protect Your Vital Targets

Yes, I know it is an obvious solution—but what I want to emphasize is that you must learn *how* to protect your vital targets. It has to become second nature. For example, keeping your chin down protects your jaw and throat. Keeping your front knee bent and turned slightly inward during stand-up fighting shields your groin area.

For power equipment drills with a training partner—ask your partner to let you know when you are failing to protect your vital targets. Make sure you know how to protect your neck and joints when the fight goes to the ground. After learning how to protect all vital targets—you should practice vital target protection during sparring in order to make sure it becomes instinctive.

Watch Out For Power Weapons

Obviously, your opponent can choose myriad techniques to attack you, but you should be most concerned with those that have the potential to inflict serious pain and damage. While a left jab might sting--it's the right cross and follow up left hook that can send you to the ground face first. You know the power weapons--so watch out for them!

Maintain Balance

It requires less force to knock someone down when they are off balance and lacking a power base.

Practice dynamic balance drills to improve your footwork so that you can always put yourself in a position of safety--just as quickly and easily as you can put yourself in a position of attack. Be sure to experiment with maintaining a power base in a variety of combat ranges.

On Contact Solutions

Strengthen Your Neck and Jaw Muscles

A fighter who cannot take a punch to the jaw is said to have a "glass jaw." Having a good chin in boxing is about being able to withstand the punishment of trading blows to the head and neck.

A strong neck helps the chin absorb some of the shock because the jaw muscles are connected to the neck muscles. A strong neck will prevent the rapid acceleration of the brain following impact from a powerful strike.

We have all seen a bout where one boxer's head is violently snapped back from the impact of a power punch. By strengthening the muscles of your neck and jaw, you can help prevent this from happening to you.

Caution: Proper form during neck exercises is essential to avoiding injury. Movements should be slow and controlled. Slowly work your way up to the recommended repetitions. Neck building exercises should be avoided if you are experiencing any neck or shoulder pain.

Neck Resistance Flexions

The best neck exercises for boxers, according to the U.S. Military Academy at West Point's intramural boxing manual, are lateral and vertical neck flexions, using a partner to create resistance.

Have a partner place his hand on your forehead with your head upright. Then try to bring your chin to your chest, pressing against the resistance of your partner's hand. Reverse the motion by having your partner place a hand on the back of your head while your chin is pressed to your chest. Then attempt to raise your head against the resistance. Repeat with resistance to moving your head to each side. Have your partner start with one hand, gently resisting your motion. Then, have your partner use two hands and more forceful opposition as your strength increases.

Neck Bridges

Lay on your back, with feet flat on the floor and shoulder-width apart, and knees bent. Press up with your thighs until you are resting on your feet and the back of your head. Slowly rock your head back all the way until your forehead reaches the mat, then rock back to the starting point. Perform 2 sets of 10-15 repetitions. You can hold a weight on your chest for added resistance as your strength increases.

Reverse Neck Bridges

The reverse neck bridge is similar to the standard neck bridge, except you will turn around so that your stomach faces the ground. Then, walk your feet forward, keeping the legs and torso straight, until your body is in a "L" configuration, with the balls of your feet and your forehead on the ground. Roll your head forward from the forehead toward the back of the head, and then back to the forehead again. Perform 2 sets of 10-15 repetitions.

Bench Neck Curls

Lay on your back on a weight bench. Then, slide your head and neck off the end of the bench, keeping it parallel to the floor--don't let it drop downward. Slowly curl your head up until your chin hits your chest, and then slowly return to the horizontal position. Perform 10-15 repetitions.

Next, lay on your stomach on the weight bench. Start with your head down, and slowly lift it until it is parallel to the ground. Perform 10-15 repetitions.

Lastly, lay on your side on the weight bench. Keep your head parallel to the ground, and lift it first to one shoulder, then lower it to the other shoulder. Flip to the other side of your body and repeat. Perform 10-15 repetitions.

Some boxers and wrestlers use a neck harness to add more weight and resistance to their neck exercises. Proper use of a neck harness will strengthen your neck, shoulder, and upper back muscles. You can check online to find and purchase a neck harness.

Isometrics

The neck can be trained with solo isometrics. Apply tension with your hands by pushing the head back.

You will resist this tension with the muscles from the neck. Isometrics can be used to train front to back (push the forehead), back to front (push the back of the head), and side-to-side (push from one side). During each exercise, you will resist the tension applied from the hands by pushing back with the muscles of the neck. Hold each exercise for 10-20 seconds.

Jaw Resistance Flexions

The following exercises will build your jaw muscles by using your hand for resistance.

Make a fist and place it below your chin. Try slowly opening your mouth while keeping pressure under your jaw. Perform 5 repetitions.

Next, open your mouth and place your thumb against one side of your chin. Then, try to push (your chin only) to the side while keeping resistance with your thumb. Repeat from the other side. Perform 5 repetitions for each side.

Lastly, open your mouth as wide as possible. Hold for 5 seconds and relax. Perform 5 repetitions.

Post-Contact Solutions

Maintain Offense

Having outstanding knockout and submission power at your disposal can go a long way toward helping you avoid knockouts and submissions. Don't become so defensive or fearful of being knocked out that you are reluctant to attack.

The reality is that you have to take some risks if you want to deliver a knockout or submission. If you are caught by a power move from your opponent--use your improved power and explosiveness to respond with overwhelming force and pressure to deter a follow-up attack. Train yourself to skillfully use power weapons for offensive attacks *and* counter attacks (in response to your opponent's offensive moves).

Chapter 9

Power Training Program

I'm sure you are ready and eager to start your power training. That's great! A strong desire to take action and implement knowledge is essential to success.

After reading this chapter, you will know how to create a personalized program for accelerated power development. Your comprehensive power program will include the following four phases:

1. Planning

2. Preparation

3. Training

4. Reviewing

Knowing how to manage all four phases of your program is the key to maximizing your innate power potential. World-class fighters understand the importance of managing and optimizing their programs through consistent planning, preparation, training, and reviewing.

Planning

Objectives

The first step in planning is to decide on the objectives. The objectives provide you with a destination. This brings focus to your training.

Having clear training objectives allows you to track and measure your progress. Without clear objectives, your training will be less productive. With clear objectives, you will see and feel progress—and real growth provides added motivation to continue growing! Don't underestimate the power of clarity.

I recommend using the S.M.A.R.T. method of goal setting to help bring clarity, power, and inspiration to your objectives. The S.M.A.R.T. acronym is broken down as follows:

S–Specific (focus the goal on a specific area; for example—punching power)

M–Measurable (quantify the goal or at least clarify the key indicator of progress; for example--the pounds of force generated by your right cross--or how many inches you can move the heavy bag with your roundhouse kick)

A–Actionable (an action-oriented goal is more effective because you can actually *do something* to achieve it)

R–Realistic (make sure the goal is attainable with reasonable, consistent action)

T–Timed (quality goals typically specify *when* the desired result will be achieved)

Use the S.M.A.R.T. goal setting method to fine-tune your objectives. It is worth the small investment of time.

Power Training Tip

I have two tips when it comes to goal setting.

1. *Avoid having too many goals at one time.* Strive for 1-3 specific training goals. I have found that having fewer goals allows me to focus and progress much faster. If I am focused on improving my throwing and takedown power--I am 100% committed to this until I reach my S.M.A.R.T. goals.

2. *Focus on micro power goals.* For example, you could focus on kinetic linking coordination--or penetration power—or timing. Focus on creating the mini-building blocks that will ultimately lead to well-rounded Combat PowerSync skills.

Commitment

The planning and achievement of a worthy goal is very fulfilling. In order to achieve your S.M.A.R.T. goals, you will need more than knowledge--and something more powerful than momentary motivation.

You will need commitment! A sincere commitment to your goals and training will drive you to take consistent action to improve. A strong commitment is far from a "wish" or "hope." It is more like an internal fire that incessantly pushes you to stay positive, focused, and moving forward toward your goals.

My belief is that you not only "want" to have knockout power. *My belief is that you are absolutely 100% "committed" to doing what it takes to have knockout power!* Please re-read the last sentence. Do you feel the same way? If so--you are committed--and your results will show it!

Personalization

As you develop your training program, be sure to personalize it in a way that works best for you. There is no one program that works for every individual. Your *ultimate power training program* must balance your aspirations, available tools, personal strengths, current weaknesses, and lifestyle requirements.

Be prepared to adjust your goals as you progress. You may have to get more or less aggressive on your goals based on results and circumstances. It's okay for your goals to flex and evolve as long as you stay committed to making consistent gains.

Time Management

Living in the 21st century has many benefits. It can also be overwhelming sometimes. For most people in developed nations, daily life continues to get more busy and complicated. We have previously unimaginable technology available to us--which should help us simplify our lives. However, more often than not—technology has the opposite effect.

In today's hyper-connected world of technology—it's easy to lose control of your time and schedule. The harder (but more satisfying) thing to do is use technology to help control your time and manage your schedule--in a way that supports your S.M.A.R.T. goals and keeps your life priorities in balance.

One of the most useful and transferrable skills for success (in anything) is time management. Developing superior fighting and knockout skills is no different. To become a more capable program planner, you will need to manage your time and schedule. Technology advances have provided very effective tools for time management.

You don't need to go "high-tech" to manage your training calendar, but if you have a mobile time management tool available to you—I suggest you take advantage of it. Above all else--I recommend keeping it simple.

If you want to make time for power training--*schedule time for power training on your calendar!* This simple action demonstrates commitment (to you--to training partners--to friends--and to family members).

Preparation

When devising your training program, you will find there are a few things that will require some preparation prior to the training sessions. These include training location, training tools, and training partners.

Location

Based on your goals, projected program, and desired training tools--you can begin to scout training facilities (unless you already have a suitable location). You should define the ideal training facility and compare your list of wants to what is readily available in your area.

First, decide if you want a formal environment--with a clear hierarchy of instructors and students. Or, perhaps you prefer a more casual environment where you can simply train without direct instruction.

Second, you should think about the facility's combat style or focus. Will it meet your power training needs? Is it a boxing gym, MMA training center, Muay Thai facility, Krav Maga class, traditional martial arts class, or simply an open gym? Of course, you may choose to visit and train in multiple facilities (if your goals require this and you can do it).

Third, you should consider the costs and facility amenities. Can you afford it? Is it clean? Is it safe? Is the equipment up-to-date and well-+maintained? If you are receiving instruction--are the instructors knowledgeable and encouraging? Always ask to speak with a few students (at varying skill levels) to get their perspective.

I suggest having an option for training at home (depending on space constraints and family considerations). Also, if you travel frequently, you should plan ahead to maintain your training while in the destination city.

Tools

To develop knockout power--you already know that you must use training tools! You simply cannot develop striking and submission power for real combat without having something to actually hit, throw, and choke with full power.

Regardless of your training location (home or away)--the availability of the power training tools covered in Chapter 6 should weigh heavily in your program preparation. If you have to purchase training tools and cannot afford multiple pieces of equipment--start with buying the most important single training tool to meet your goals. You can save money by searching for pre-owned combat training equipment on Craig's List®, Amazon®, and eBay®.

Partners

Solo training is a viable solution for improving your combat attributes. However, to fully develop your fighting skills--you will need capable training partners who are willing to help you.

Effective training partners can be equally skilled—more skilled—or even less skilled than you. They do not (necessarily) have to share your specific goals, but a good training partner will respect and support your goals. Of course, you should reciprocate by providing training assistance and encouragement to your partners.

When I refer to training partners, I am also including coaches and instructors (the best will consider themselves lifelong students and willing training partners). An experienced and caring combat instructor or coach can help you identify and solve the "gaps" in your training program.

Training

Programs

You have completed the planning and preparation phases—and you are ready to create the specific training programs that will produce your knockout power. I suggest you document your training program. You can choose to use a digital or paper solution. I keep my training program information on a cloud storage server--so that I can conveniently access it anytime from my laptop or smart phone. For me, this works because I can easily capture new training ideas--and review or change my program as needed.

You (and your instructor or training partners) will ultimately need to create your specific (ideal) power training program. To help you get started--I will provide a framework that has proven itself to be a helpful tool for many combat students. The power program framework consists of the following four categories:

1. Fitness

2. Attributes

3. Skills

4. Fighting

Fitness: This category focuses on fitness, health, and nutrition. *Strength and stamina should be the areas of emphasis for a power student.* A healthy diet is important for optimal health and energy to maintain a rigorous training program.

Don't forget to include short but specific mental training drills (meditation, visualization, and self-hypnosis) as part of your regular program.

Attributes: Combat attributes refer to the qualities and fundamental capabilities of a fighter. Some fighters (with adequate attributes) are able to compensate for a lack of technique or experience. I recall one unique student who had naturally high levels of both speed *and* power. Despite his very limited technical skill and experience (he was new to combat sports)--he was consistently winning against some of the more experienced students in the class because of his superior *attributes*.

Because your goal is to maximize the attribute of power--I recommend viewing power as the *macro attribute* in your training--and all other attributes can be considered *micro attributes*, which form the vital support network for your Combat PowerSync. You are simply clarifying that power is the *primary* training attribute.

Combat power micro attributes (see Chapter 4) include the following:

*Balance

*Speed

*Timing

*Distance

*Accuracy

*Strength

*Stamina

Every one of these attributes has a specific role and will contribute to the development of your knockout power. In your training, I encourage you to consistently push to identify and use the most effective tools, drills, and partners for maximizing these attributes.

Skills: Skill (acquired through experience and training) is the learned ability to consistently carry out a task with pre-determined results.

More specifically, skill in fighting is the ability to successfully execute offensive, defensive, and counter maneuvers to attain victory (as defined by the rules of the combat situation). Skill is concerned with technical proficiency or ability more than raw attribute levels. It is developed through expanded knowledge of fighting techniques, movement repetition, improved coordination, and fighting experience.

Understanding that you should always counter "technique A" with "technique B" is not something you will know just because you have superior strength. You must develop superior *skills* in fighting to optimize your Combat PowerSync.

The best way to develop superior fighting skills is to master the most effective offensive, defensive, and counter techniques from a variety of realistic combat systems. This cross-training approach is critical to the development of your Combat

PowerSync--and your ability to deliver knockout power against any opponent or style of fighting.

Fighting: The fourth category of the power training program framework is fighting. This includes contact sparring, self-defense simulations, and competitive bouts.

Contact fighting develops your ability to synthesize and apply your conditioning, attributes, and skills against a real opponent. Obviously, every combat power student should include contact fighting (with appropriate gear) in his training program.

As discussed earlier in this book, there are several fighting drills that you (and your partners) can incorporate---from light contact sparring---to full-contact situational fighting.

Power Training Tip

Don't ever lose sight of the fact that training itself must become a consistent habit if you want to develop advanced combat power. Take active steps to avoid boredom and maintain your commitment. Champion fighters use a variety of strategies and tools to stay motivated and engaged, including: music, new equipment, new drills, new partners, and planned breaks to help revitalize their training. Do what you need to do to keep your workouts fresh and productive.

Reviewing

You have just finished a great workout. Your training partners are starting to take notice of your increasing power. So, what's next? Well, for starters--don't simply disengage until the next workout. Between training sessions--you should review your progress and make necessary adjustments to your program.

Regular performance reviews are an integral part of all world-class training and development programs. Superstar professional athletes have access to sophisticated equipment and dedicated personnel for this phase of their training program. You really don't need expensive tools or a bevy of assistant coaches—but you do need to *review your power program regularly for continuous improvement.*

I have witnessed many combat students break through previous plateaus and elevate their fighting attributes to new, higher levels after getting serious about program reviews. I'm sure you will do the same. It only requires 5 – 15 minutes of your time between workouts.

Training Journal

A training journal is an indispensable tool for the serious fighter. With the help of a training journal--

you can eliminate unproductive activity--and increase the focus on drills and tools that are delivering the greatest improvements and results.

What you actually record in your training journal is up to you. It depends on your S.M.A.R.T. goals and which components of Combat PowerSync you are focused on developing. I suggest keeping it simple and short--so that you will actually do it (record progress) regularly.

Some of the program review information in my training journal includes: date, training category, duration, training tool, power component, current weight, power weapons emphasized, progress on key metrics, training partners, and pertinent comments (suggestions for improvement, general observations, etc.)

You can choose to use a paper journal or digital journal on your smart phone (or computer). The key is to be consistent and accurate in your program reviews. Personally, I like to conduct my program reviews immediately after each workout. I have found that this works best for me because the training outcomes are still fresh in my mind—and I can preview and prepare for the next workout.

Video

Occasionally, I will record videos of my training sessions. The feedback provided by video is very helpful. It can provide a coach's perspective. Video reviews of your training sessions will help you validate areas of improvement and identify areas of opportunity.

To start, you can record short videos of your training when you are working on specific drills or components of power. You can use a smart phone, camera (with a video feature), or a video recorder. After reviewing your training videos—I suggest you capture any key observations in your training journal.

Body Awareness

In addition to using training journals and video recordings--you must *tune in to your instincts for subconscious training guidance*. I am always amazed by the breakthrough solutions and answers I receive when I am attuned to my body, mind, and emotions.

Always listen closely to your body for signals to push harder or hold back in your training. Develop heightened body awareness. You will improve faster and avoid setbacks due to injuries.

Sample Program

A comprehensive combat power program is built on five distinct categories. These include: fitness, attributes, skills, and fighting. The fifth category is education—which includes knowledge, inspiration, and program management (planning, preparation, and reviewing).

To assist you in the creation of your power training program--I have provided a sample program. It is simply a starting point. I strongly recommend that you adapt and personalize the program to align with your goals, needs, and schedules.

Fitness

*Weight Training (1-2x weekly)

*Cardio Training--Aerobic and Anaerobic; Power Lung (3-5x weekly)

*Nutrition--Healthy Diet and Supplements (daily)

*Meditation (3-6x weekly)

*Power Breathing (3-6x weekly)

*Neck and Jaw Strengthening (1-2x weekly)

*Stretching (3-5x weekly)

Attributes Training

>   *Torquing Drills or Paper Target

>   *Heavy Bag or Punching Dummy

>   *Shadow Fighting or Resistance Bands

>   *Pads/Shields or Focus Mitts

>   *Double End Bag or Reflex Bag

>   *Grappling Dummy or Medicine Ball

Skills Training

>   *Power Strikes

>   *Power Throws

>   *Power Takedowns

>   *Power Chokes

>   *Power Locks

>   *Vital Targets

>   *Defensive Maneuvers

>   *Cross-style Training

Fighting

>   *Full Speed Contact Sparring

*Half Speed Non-contact Sparring

*Situational Contact Sparring

*Striking-focused Sparring

*Grappling-focused Sparring

*Range-specific Sparring (refer to Combat Range Matrix)

*Footwork Sparring

*Blind Sparring

I suggest you re-read the section on "5 classifications of combat power development training" from Chapter 2. It will help you create an effective and balanced training program based on your experience and skill level—plus, availability of partners and tools.

Power Training Tip

Try to maintain *weekly balance* in your combat power training by including drills or exercises for every category (fitness, attributes, skills, and fighting). If you have limited time for training during a hectic week— try to plan that limited time so that you can *make progress* (or at least maintain progress) in all categories. Try to avoid regressing in any one training category because it could have a negative impact on your total combat power.

During particularly busy weeks, you may find that you only have 15 minutes for each training category. Don't stress. Just make sure your training time is always productive and enjoyable. Also, create a plan and schedule for the following week that allows more time for training and improvement.

Chapter 10

Combat Power Inspiration

In this chapter, you will learn how to maintain your power training motivation by studying knockout and submission masters--building a support team--and becoming a super learner.

Power Masters

A power fighter with superior knockout or submission skills is usually one of three types:

1. Speed-based power fighter

2. Strength-based power fighter

3. Mechanics-based power fighter

Speed-based power fighters deliver knockout strikes and submissions that very often catch the opponent by surprise. Strength-based power fighters use their physical strength to deliver knockout strikes and submissions with deeply penetrating force. Lastly, mechanics-based power fighters depend on superior technique and kinetic linking to deliver knockout strikes and winning submissions.

The following fighters are recognized by most experts as having world-class combat power. These fighters--from a variety of combat styles—have displayed superior power and ability to knock out or incapacitate opponents. Their weapon of choice varies from stunning punches--to devastating kicks--to debilitating takedowns and submissions.

I encourage you to study these (and other) champion power fighters. Use them as inspiration and constant motivation to help you maximize your personal combat power.

The list is in no particular order. Enjoy the videos!

Sugar Ray Robinson

The original "Sugar" Ray is widely considered the #1 boxer of all time.

Power Type: Speed *and* strength-based. Plus, great mechanics.

Specialty: Boxing; Punching

Video Highlights: http://goo.gl/iYevgz

Rocky Marciano

Retired with a perfect 49 wins and 0 losses, with 43 wins by knockout.

> Power Type: Mechanics-based.

> Specialty: Boxing; Punching

> Video Highlights: http://goo.gl/MBSBM7

Joe Louis

The "Brown Bomber" is regarded by many as the #1 heavyweight boxer of all time, having successfully defended his heavyweight title a record 25 times.

> Power Type: Speed *and* strength-based.

> Specialty: Boxing; Punching

> Video Highlights: http://goo.gl/vQCkDx

Roy Jones Jr.

One of the best pound for pound boxers of the modern era.

> Power Type: Speed-based.

> Specialty: Boxing; Punching

> Video Highlights: http://goo.gl/RgaxV0

Mike Tyson

At 20 years old, "Iron Mike" was the youngest undisputed heavyweight champion.

> Power Type: Strength-based.
>
> Specialty: Boxing; Punching
>
> Video Highlights: http://goo.gl/mjPJEx

Anderson Silva

The "Spider" is generally considered the best MMA fighter of all time and holds the longest title defense streak in UFC history.

> Power Type: Speed *and* strength-based. Plus, great mechanics. Exemplifies Combat PowerSync.
>
> Specialty: MMA; Striking
>
> Video Highlights: http://goo.gl/yHzBpk

Georges St. Pierre

"Rush" holds the record for most wins in UFC history (19), and he is considered (by most experts) to be the #2 greatest MMA fighter of all-time.

> Power Type: Strength-based.
>
> Specialty: MMA; Grappling and Striking

Video Highlights: http://goo.gl/lGeDJO

Mirko Filipovic

"Cro Crop" is considered one of the most powerful kickers of all time. He famously described his left round kick to the head as "right leg, hospital; left leg, cemetery."

Power Type: Strength-based.

Specialty: MMA; Striking

Video Highlights: http://goo.gl/kEBEfi

Royce Gracie

Winner of UFC 1-4, Gracie revolutionized mixed martial arts and popularized grappling. He holds the record for most consecutive submission victories in UFC history (11).

Power Type: Mechanics-based.

Specialty: MMA; Grappling

Video Highlights: http://goo.gl/aOlnVG

Lucia Rijker

Dubbed "The Most Dangerous Woman in the World," Rijker became the first female inducted into the Boxing Hall of Fame, with a 17-0 record (14 by KO). In addition, she has a Muay Thai record of 37-0 (25 KOs).

Power Type: Mechanics-based.

Specialty: MMA; Striking

Video Highlights: http://goo.gl/GAoPAE

Ronda Rousey

"Rowdy" b.k.a. the "Armbar Assassin" is the current #1 female MMA fighter in the world, and the first woman to sign a contract with the UFC. She has defeated all of her opponents by submission with an arm bar.

Power Type: Mechanics-based.

Specialty: MMA; Grappling

Video Highlights: http://goo.gl/736hPX

Bruce Lee

One of the most influential martial artist of all time and often cited as the father of mixed martial arts and modern training methods.

Power Type: Speed-based.

Specialty: Mixed Martial Arts; Striking

Video Highlights: http://goo.gl/4YhiaY

Combat Power Team

Becoming a superior power fighter (in combat sports or self-defense) requires dedication and consistent training. My guess is that you are a self-motivated person (as evidenced by the fact that you are reading this guide).

The greatest gains in self-improvement are achieved when internal motivation and consistent action is complemented with a strong support network. If you want to maximize your combat power--you should actively work to build and maintain a network of people who can aid you in developing knockout power.

Your *combat power team* can include the following:

*Training partners

*Coaches

*Instructors

*Consultants

*Role models

*Online communities (forums, blogs, social media groups)

*Family

*Friends

*Fans

*Sponsors

Don't underestimate the power of having a capable and caring team to help you achieve your goals. You don't need a large or formal team. But, your combat power team members *must* be supportive and (hopefully) provide clear benefits--such as knowledge, inspiration, critical feedback, tools, or monetary support.

To get the most value from a combat power team--*be sure to reciprocate by regularly thanking and supporting helpful team members.*

Also, as your knowledge and skills improve, you will gain more opportunities to mentor and educate other combat students. Don't miss these opportunities. It is really true--*"teaching is one of the best ways to learn."*

Combat Power Student

The most accomplished and respected fighters are typically serious students of the combat arts. This notion applies to any field or discipline. The best of the best in sports, military, business, medicine, science, teaching, and entertainment are typically the most fervent students.

Commit yourself to continuous improvement and evolution as a combat student. If you are not already--I encourage you to become a perennial student of combat power training.

Continual education will help you stay engaged and motivated. This is the fifth category of power training. You will discover new innovations, game-changing tools, and new sources of inspiration.

Don't let your combat knowledge stagnate. Invest in learning tools--such as instructional books, videos, and seminars. The master combat student will continuously adapt his fighting strategies and training methods based on simple science and practical knowledge.

Superior fighters are superior learners!

Conclusion

Final Thoughts on Power Training

Congratulations! You have completed the study of Combat Power Training. For fast results, start applying this information and incorporating the Combat PowerSync principles into your regular training. You will be delighted by the transformation in your total power and fighting ability.

Reading this book will not turn you into the greatest knockout artist on earth. However, if you use the drills, exercises, and information as instructed-- you will significantly improve your fighting power for competition and self-defense. Consistent application of the information contained in this guide is guaranteed to double your power and help you become the best fighter you can be.

By covering one specific attribute, combat power, in great detail--my goal is to keep this book distinguished and highly regarded. My mission is to maintain the highest standard of quality by offering specialized combat training information that is simple, innovative, affordable, and highly effective in helping you achieve your goals.

Train Hard. Win Easy.

J. Barnes

http://www.CombatTrainingBooks.com

Connect with J. Barnes

If you have questions or comments on combat training, please feel free to contact me.

jbarnes@combattrainingbooks.com

More Books by J. Barnes

Speed Training for Combat, Boxing, Martial Arts, and MMA: How to Maximize Your Hand Speed, Foot Speed, Punching Speed, Kicking Speed, Wrestling Speed, and Fighting Speed - Available Now!

http://goo.gl/ZdXPJr

Mental Training for Combat Warriors: How to Meditate and Maximize Killer Instinct for Success in Combat, MMA, Boxing, Wrestling, Martial Arts and Self-Defense - Available 2014

Visit my author page below and sign up under "Stay Up To Date" to receive an email when I release new books. http://goo.gl/SBMufM

Or, send an email, and I will personally notify you when this book is released. jbarnes@combattrainingbooks.com

Pressure Points for Fighting, Self Defense, and Martial Arts: How to Strike Vital Targets and Win Fights Quickly - Available 2014

Visit my author page below and sign up under "Stay Up To Date" to receive an email when I release new books. http://goo.gl/SBMufM

Or, send an email, and I will personally notify you when this book is released.
jbarnes@combattrainingbooks.com

Thank You

My sincere thanks to you for purchasing and reading this book. If you are satisfied with this book, please take a moment to leave a helpful review on Amazon.

Your feedback is greatly appreciated, and it will help me continue to write books that help you get results and achieve your goals.

CPSIA information can be obtained at www.ICGtesting.com
Printed in the USA
LVOW06s1611071015

457323LV00002B/299/P